HELLO JUNK MAIL!

by Jed L. Nancy™

Other Books Ted L. Nancy Also Wrote:

Letters From A Nut

More Letters From A Nut

Extra Nutty! Even More Letters From A Nut

Published by National Lampoon Press

National Lampoon, Inc. • 8228 Sunset Boulevard • Los Angeles • CA 90046 • USA

AMEX:NLN

NATIONAL LAMPOON, NATIONAL LAMPOON PRESS and colophon are trademarks of National Lampoon

Hello junk mail
/ by Ted L. Nancy -- 1st ed.

p. cm.

ISBN-10: 0980059216
ISBN-13: 978-0980059212 $17.95

Cover Design by
Alan Marder and Marty Dundics

Illustrations by
Alan Marder

Book Design by
JKNaughton

BY WAY OF INTRODUCTION...

Hello. It's me, Ted L. Nancy. Let me just tell you what I have been doing. I have befriended a foreign family living in Glendale. Here is what happened:

My first contact with the Kabobby family was the night of August 30, 2004. I went to a Papaya Stand to pick up some squishy juice for a friend who had bladder symptoms. (He made a strange noise which today is still unidentifiable.) We were going to watch *American Gladiators* later on TV and I was to monitor his bladder while he drank squishy juice with papaya particles in it.

When I got home I noticed a strange pair of men's underwear on my clothesline which threw me into a silent rage. I belched up a plum and barked out the name Otto.

Let me just explain here: I had been at my summer home in Glendale, California, a community of mostly foreign people and parrots. I like to relax in the summer with foreign people. They are very relaxing, mostly in the summer. When I saw this large pair of men's underwear (blue with unchecked boxes on them) on my clothesline I realized a new family had moved in next door and had taken the liberty to dry out a pair of their underwear on my clothesline which is in my front yard.

I took the underwear off the clothesline, attempted to photoshop my dog, and along with a fruitcake went next door to introduce myself and welcome these new neighbors to the neighborhood. I rang their doorbell. That is when I first met the Kabobby family of Glendale.

I was invited in and I gave them back their underwear and we all shared some of my fruitcake in their living room of their small home. I noticed that Geela Kabobby had a pile of Junk Mail on her coffee table. They were typical Junk Mail letters - from mortgage companies and credit cards - with all kinds of offers for the Kabobby family. I said, "Boy you really have a pile of Junk Mail there on your coffee table."

She explained that this pile is all of the mail they received since they moved into their new home. They were so excited that someone in America was writing to them. And that each family member wanted to write back to the Junk Mailers and answer these letters. ROY! Excuse me here. But I have a disease which causes me to bark out men's names. I am currently being treated with Canadian Internet knockoff drugs.

I looked over this pile of mail and thought, *I don't know what this is, but it's some pretty powerful stuff.*

When I left, I asked Hamooli Kabobby if we could get together again and try answering some of this Junk Mail. He said okay and over the next couple of weeks we did just that. I went back over to the Kabobby house - which is right next door to my summer home - and I asked Grandfather Bahir Kabobby, Hamooli's father, if he had any more Junk Mail. He said, "Sure, there is a lot more. That's all we get in the mail - is this junk!"

I sat down with the entire Kabobby Family: Hamooli Kabobby, his wife Geela, their children Scott, daughters Tahini, and Baby Maheeni, Grandfather Bahir and various other relatives. And I proclaimed: "We must answer this Junk Mail. We must write back! They are expecting answers - let us write them!" Then I showed everybody a photoshop picture of my dog. (To great delight.)

Now, me being a letter writer, I decided to help this family in answering this Junk Mail. I think I am pretty good at this, answering letters, plus I like Kabobs - so why not? Huh? So with all the intelligence I have, I helped these people. They spoke poor English and did not understand the fine ways of mail. I have guided them through the letter-writing. Besides, I like to help foreign people whenever I get a chance. Once a family helped me in Baznatti when I was traveling and needed assistance with a welt.

I have now read the letters to various people I know whose tolerance of Junk Mail and offers in general have been rigorously developed to professional strength. They all liked this various Junk Mail. ANDY!

Then I called my literary agent - Dan Strone, formerly of the William Morris Agency and now the head of Trident Literary Agency, an extremely charming and well dressed man, and more importantly, one of the smartest guys in show business. I said, "Dan, I have a bunch of letters here that I think could be some kind of book if you could get enough of them." So Dan got an outfit together and a lunch was arranged. When you give something good to Dan Strone it's like handing the ball off to Peyton Manning. You just know it's going places.

I will say the Kabobbys possess many of the qualities I consider for a good life. They enjoy the simple things. Like weird cruises, Bounce Fabric Freshener sheets, and rash ointments. They are a decent family. I guess I would like to say the Kabobby family is like yours and my family. We all get endless amounts of Junk Mail. And we usually throw it away. I guess I would like to say that. (That they are like yours and my family.) But I can't. The Kabobbys are not like you or me. They did not throw their Junk Mail away. They answered it. Who does that?

So I knew from the beginning that I had to do everything I could to let as many people as possible read the hilarious truth about what has been going on inside the mailbox of the Kabobbys Of Glendale, a newly arrived foreign family. And my new neighbors. TITO!

Jed L. Nancy

THE KABOBBY HOUSE IS IN TROUBLE

TERMINIX
No Bugs. No Hassles.

GET THE FACTS ABOUT TERMITES—WHAT YOU DON'T KNOW COULD BE DAMAGING.

Hamooli Kabobby
1413 1/2 W. Kenneth Rd. # 193
Glendale, CA 91201-1478

I need termite facts!

Call 1-800-TERMINIX (1-800-837-6464)
for a FREE termite inspection
and SAVINGS of up to 20%!

Dear Hamooli Kabobby,

When it comes to protecting one of your biggest investments, your home, you don't want to make any mistakes. Yet, what you don't know about termites could put your home and your finances at risk.

Count on Terminix to help keep you informed so that you can make the best decision to guard yourself against these destructive insects.

Uh oh! Problem

FACT: Even if a home has been previously treated for termites, it could still be at risk.

Termites are relentless in their search for food. And once they've visited your home, they may return to the familiar site over and over again. Ongoing professional service is the best way to combat these persistent foragers.

FACT: Nationally, termites cause $2 billion in home damage and repair costs every year.

Now that you know the facts about subterranean termites, make the best decision for your home and your finances. For quality termite service from the nation's leader in termite control and *Unlimited Lifetime Protection*, choose Terminix.

Sincerely,

Your Terminix Manager

- 2 -

HAMOOLI KABOBBY
1413 1/2 Kenneth Rd.
#193
Glendale, CA 91201

TERMINIX MGT
TERMINIX PEST CONTROL
P.O. Box 3300
Memphis, TN 38173

Dear Mr. John Mgt of the Terminix Peoples,

First let me thank you for sending me mail. Especially about
termites. Many of the things that you say in your letter to me
are true: Termites are relentless in their search for food. Yes!
Who isn't? I am hungry right now. (I may snack) You say my home
could still be at risk. From what? Let me tell you about myself:

My name is Hamooli Kabobby. My wife is Geela. We have 3
children. Daughter Tahini, 16, Son Razi or "Scott", 20, as we
call him here in U.S., and baby Maheeni. She is 39 months and
weighs 125. She eats 6 inch subs from the Subway. We live in
Glendale, California. I am originally from Barzania. (A small
village but filled with termites)

When I got your offer in mail I was interested. Why? I have a
pest leeching off me now. He is cousin Shwarmi who will be
visiting soon. In my country, he is considered a feezi. Do you
know what a feezi is? It is a tick that suckles and bleeds dry
one until the arm is swollen and useless! HASSEAMM!!! SALEELAM,
SALEELAM!! I dread Shwarmi's visit tomorrow. He is termite!

Now down to your offer: Yes i am interested! How can we work
together to remove: Your termites. From: My house. Please
correspond and we can continue to upgrade our relationship.

Thank you for your mail, Mr. John Mgt, of Terminix Termite Co I
am very, very interested. (That is 2 verys.) How will I pay for
this? I have no money.

Respectfully,

Hamooli Kabobby

Platinum Plus® Credit Card	
Customer:	Hamooli Kabobby
Credit Line:	**As High as $100,000**
APR:	**0% Introductory Fixed APR† for cash advance checks and balance transfers until January 2007**
Annual Fee:	**None**
Apply Toll-free:	**Call 1-866-598-4970 for an instant decision. Approved cards mailed within 48 hours.**

************AUTO** 3-DIGIT 912
32720692337 LMOY TV-404 9Q
Hamooli Kabobby
1413 1/2 W Kenneth Rd Apt 193
Glendale CA 91201-1478

Dear Hamooli Kabobby,

I am pleased to present you with an opportunity that will save you money—the no-annual-fee MBNA® Platinum Plus® Visa® credit card. This program offers several money-saving features like:

need BAdLy

> **An Introductory 0% Fixed♦ Annual Percentage Rate (APR)†** for cash advance checks and balance transfers until your statement closing date in January 2007, when you use the MBNA Platinum Plus Visa credit card.

This Introductory APR applies only to cash advance checks and balance transfers and may end sooner if your account is paid late. For retail purchases, you'll also enjoy a great APR right from the start. (Please note that payments are applied first to balances with the lowest APR.) You can take immediate advantage of this great offer with an instant decision on your request—call toll-free **1-866-598-4970** today. (TTY users, see below) And as much as you'll enjoy the savings of your new MBNA Platinum Plus credit card—that's just the beginning of the benefits you'll enjoy!

For example, our Platinum Plus credit lines may go as high as $100,000. You can access your account through your card, cash advance checks, or at hundreds of thousands of ATMs around the world. Emergency card replacement, zero liability for fraudulent charges, and Common Carrier Travel Accident Insurance coverage are just a few of the features of this account.** The Platinum Plus card also gives you full access to world-class travel planning services. One toll-free call puts you in touch with travel specialists with insights into some of the world's best getaways.

Customer service specialists are available 24 hours a day, every day of the year to meet your needs. These specialists are ready to instantly respond to your credit line increase request, help resolve disputes with merchants, and answer any questions you may have. They will also contact you if they detect unusual activity on your account.

The highest credit line available . . . a great introductory 0% APR for cash advance checks and balance transfers until January 2007†. . . No Annual Fee . . . around-the-clock Customer service . . . these add up to the best value in premium cards today.

Just complete and return the attached Personal Request Form. Or with your request form handy, call toll-free 1-866-598-4970 to request your card today. (TTY users, call 1-800-833-6262.) You can even get an instant decision Monday–Friday, 9 a.m.–9 p.m., Eastern time, and upon approval, your card could be on its way within 48 hours.

Sincerely,

Director of Marketing, MBNA America

P.S. Take full advantage of the Introductory **0%** APR for cash advance checks and balance transfers **until January 2007**.† Plus, you can get a great APR for retail purchases right from the start!

HAMOOLI KABOBBY
1413 1/2 Kenneth Rd.
#193
Glendale, CA 91201

J (PERSON)
PLATINUM PLUS CREDIT CARD
P.O. Box 22011
Wilmington, Delaware 19891-0011

Dear J (Person) of Platinum Plus Credit Card Peoples:

What a relief to receive this very generous offer from you for
credit card. I was just approached by Mr. John Mgt of Terminix
Peoples. He wants to termite my house and it is costly to be
sure. Your offer of $100,000.00 (72 million shookas Belzarian
money) is outstanding. That is exactly cost of termite
infestation fee so this will come in handy. When can I get? I
need it now!!! (Call me Andy if we ever meet! I am serious I
like name)

Let me further tell you about me. My wife Geela is a fine woman.
But I do not need fine woman. I need understanding woman (I
would also like hottie). Geela is neither. I need someone who
will not judge me for some odors which I may have. Yes, I am a
foreigner and some foreigners have odor. KALLELAM! MAHATZEE!
But Geela is going too far. If it's not my foul breath, it's my
body stench. If it's not my toe fungoo, it's whole foot. And
what is wrong with my teeth? Recently we went to Sherman
Willhelms Paint Store and I showed Geela on paint chart color of
my teeth and how popular beige is. Does she care? No! That is
what I mean by not being understanding. (And she is not hottie)
KOOTRILAM!!! SALEEUMM!! I CURSE ALL SHERMAN WILLHELMS PAINT
CHARTS!!!

So, I say to you, J of Platinum Plus Credit Card peoples: Lets
get me that money soon, and get rid of my termites!!! (That is 3
exclamation points) When can I get it? The money? How soon? I
need it now! My house is being eaten.

With Farzanian Respect,

Hamooli Kabobby

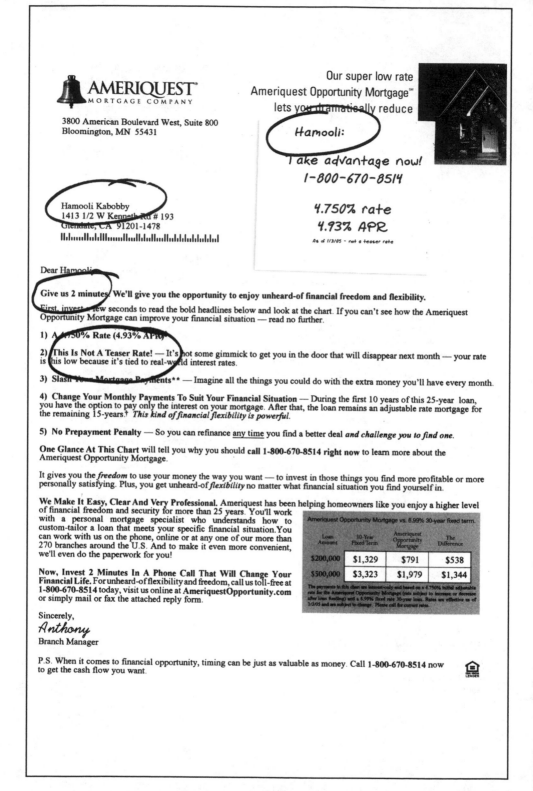

AMERIQUEST
MORTGAGE COMPANY

3800 American Boulevard West, Suite 800
Bloomington, MN 55431

Our super low rate
Ameriquest Opportunity Mortgage℠
lets you dramatically reduce

Hamooli:

Take advantage now!
1-800-670-8514

4.750% rate
4.93% APR

As of 1/3/05 - not a teaser rate

Hamooli Kabobby
1413 1/2 W Kenneth Rd # 193
Glendale, CA 91201-1478

Dear Hamooli:

Give us 2 minutes. We'll give you the opportunity to enjoy unheard-of financial freedom and flexibility.

First, invest a few seconds to read the bold headlines below and look at the chart. If you can't see how the Ameriquest Opportunity Mortgage can improve your financial situation — read no further.

1) A **4.750% Rate (4.93% APR)**.

2) **This Is Not A Teaser Rate!** — It's not some gimmick to get you in the door that will disappear next month — your rate is this low because it's tied to real-world interest rates.

3) **Slash Your Mortgage Payments**** — Imagine all the things you could do with the extra money you'll have every month.

4) **Change Your Monthly Payments To Suit Your Financial Situation** — During the first 10 years of this 25-year loan, you have the option to pay only the interest on your mortgage. After that, the loan remains an adjustable rate mortgage for the remaining 15-years.† *This kind of financial flexibility is powerful.*

5) **No Prepayment Penalty** — So you can refinance <u>any time</u> you find a better deal *and challenge you to find one.*

One Glance At This Chart will tell you why you should **call 1-800-670-8514 right now** to learn more about the Ameriquest Opportunity Mortgage.

It gives you the *freedom* to use your money the way you want — to invest in those things you find more profitable or more personally satisfying. Plus, you get unheard-of *flexibility* no matter what financial situation you find yourself in.

We Make It Easy, Clear And Very Professional. Ameriquest has been helping homeowners like you enjoy a higher level of financial freedom and security for more than 25 years. You'll work with a personal mortgage specialist who understands how to custom-tailor a loan that meets your specific financial situation. You can work with us on the phone, online or at any one of our more than 270 branches around the U.S. And to make it even more convenient, we'll even do the paperwork for you!

Now, Invest 2 Minutes In A Phone Call That Will Change Your Financial Life. For unheard-of flexibility and freedom, call us toll-free at 1-800-670-8514 today, visit us online at **AmeriquestOpportunity.com** or simply mail or fax the attached reply form.

Ameriquest Opportunity Mortgage vs. 6.99% 30-year fixed term.

Loan Amount	30-Year Fixed Term	Ameriquest Opportunity Mortgage	The Difference
$200,000	$1,329	$791	$538
$500,000	$3,323	$1,979	$1,344

The payments in this chart are interest-only and based on a 4.750% initial adjustable rate for the Ameriquest Opportunity Mortgage (rate subject to increase or decrease after loan funding) and a 6.99% fixed rate 30-year loan. Rates are effective as of 1/3/05 and are subject to change. Please call for current rates.

Sincerely,

Anthony
Branch Manager

P.S. When it comes to financial opportunity, timing can be just as valuable as money. Call **1-800-670-8514** now to get the cash flow you want.

EQUAL HOUSING LENDER

HAMOOLI KABOBBY
1413 1/2 Kenneth Rd.
#193
Glendale, CA 91201

Anthony (Person)
AMERIQUEST MORTGAGE CO.
3800 American Blvd West, Suite 800
Bloomington, MN 55431

My Dear Anthony People:

Listen to me. Yes, I need new home loan. NOW!!! My house
collapsed!!! From the termites. They are bastards. The whole
thing went down like cheap mall shelving. I was sitting in my
underwear enjoying humus and Carrs wafers with Cousin Shwarmi and
son Scott when we heard tiny gnawing. Shwarmi said "Is that tiny
gnawing I hear?" I said "Yes. I have been hearing it for some
time now. I am waiting for $100,000. from J & the Platinum
peoples and it should arrive soon." Shwarmi said "Is that the
same Platinum peoples that have titty bar on Floog Avenue in
Burbank?" (I curse this man under my tongue for: his pock marked
skin & veiny arms)

Tiny gnawing continued as Shwarmi jabbered on about his visits to
Platinum club and how he had his "eye" on Jennifer Lopez type. He
said he spent $500.00 on lap dance. Hah! This with him mooching
me for Carrs wafers & humus. I curse his skin tag & 1 thick
eyebrow. (He also strung a twine across my car to dry his sock
on) he is a feezi!

In your mail you ask for 2 minutes. I give it to you, Mr. A. For
what I do not know. I will be candid and up front with you. When
you say THIS IS NOT A TEASER RATE (In bold) what do you mean? In
my country bold mean something to stand out. What is standing out
here? DO NOT TEASE ME! (Unless you are hottie; female please; no
exceptions) Now down to mortgage situation: Of course I am
looking for unheard of financial flexibility. Because the ones I
heard of I don't like! I have no house left. It is a pile of
gnawed wood. And to make matters worse I have no job. I did not
want to tell you this because it could affect my loan. When can I
get loan? Let's communicate in Bazzarian.

Sincerely,

Hamooli Kabobby
Unemployed, broke, man with no home (Write me)

- 7 -

HAMOOLI KABOBBY
1413 1/2 Kenneth Rd.
#193
Glendale, CA 91201

Subscriptions
COUNTRY MAGAZINE
P/O. Box 994
Greendale, WI 53129-0994

Dear Country Magazine Peoples:

Hello! And thank you for generous offer of umbrella. I need
umbrella. Why? Because I have no house. It collapsed. It went
down like cheap Chinese kite. So a covering on my head is
welcome. And 40 foot of umbrella will cover my whole family. By
the way, what Country is your magazine about?

Let me now tell you about Grandfather Bahir who is living in
refrigerator carton in my backyard. He arrived from Sazznassian.
He is 80 years old but still drives a snow plow. Yesterday he
took snow plow out and on asphalt street snow plowed many cars in
his way. (One was Toyota) But there is no snow in Glendale to
buffer cars from being hit. So there was metal screeching.

When I go to my backyard and see Grandfather Bahir in cardboard
refrigerator container cooking and washing his underwear out I am
saddened. HE IS MY GRANDFATHER FOR GOD'S SAKE!! I want to put
him under this umbrella. HOLILAM, HASHEEUM!! BAHIR!!

I notice in your ad you say your umbrella opens to full 40 feet
but is small enough to fit in my pocket. You are comparing figs
to olives. Who are you kidding? When is my magazine coming? I
am anxious to read it then reread it again. HALILAMM!! (Call me
Roy if we ever meet. I need that)

Please reply with how I may get my magazine and umbrella delivered
soon. I am anxious.

With respect & dignity,

Hamooli Kabobby
Hamooli Kabobby

Country

P.O. Box 5294
Harlan, IA 51593-0794

February 21, 2007

||l.....||..|.|||.....||...|l.|..||...|l.|.|.|..|.|..|.|..|
Hamooli Kobobby
No 193
1413 1/2 Kenneth Rd
Glendale, CA 91201-1478

Account #: COU

Dear Customer:

We have received your inquiry regarding your subscription to *COUNTRY*. At
this time we are unable to address your concerns without further information.

If possible please send your account number. It is located just above your
name and address on your mailing label.

Please provide a brief summary of your original inquiry. Your reply will
receive our immediate attention.

Customer Service

129707943/HPCG/BR2

HAMOOLI KABOBBY
1413 1/2 Kenneth Rd.
#193
Glendale, CA 91201

Dear Country Magazine,

Thank you for writing RE: My Umbrella and Country Magazine. I am
long time Country Magazine reader. In my country it's all I read.
I was happy to receive your Umbrella offer. Now that is not
coming too? So now I have no Umbrella and no magazine?

You tell em to send you brief summary of original inquiry. In
original inquiry I mention Grandfather Bahir. He drives snow
plow. (Toyota problem) he cooks food in his carton, washes
underpants. Umbrella is for entire family for mass covering. I
told you all this. Is there any other colors besides blue for
Umbrella? (purple???) Where is:

my Umbrella
my Magazine

Hamooli Kabobby

- 12 -

HAMOOLI KABOBBY
1413 1/2 Kenneth Rd.
#193
Glendale, CA 91201

Miss Connie
PENN FOSTER CAREER SCHOOL
926 Oak St.
Scranton, PA 18515

Hello Miss Connie & Penn Foster Career School!

Thank you for congratulating me on being **PRE-APPROVED IN THE AT-HOME CAREER TRAINING PROGRAM** at Penn Foster Freeze Career school. I need job! I have heard many things about Penn Foster. Some good. So when this offer came in and with my current poor situation, I was intrigued. Please excuse my English as I have only lived here short time and I suffer from Harn's Shouts. (I bark out Middle Eastern foods from my last job.)

Now down to my career: In my country I was G-4 L7 Grade 19b organizer in food industry. I did for 34 years, working in food industry in accounting position. I have 24 years of mathematics specializing in Yuro numbers in the dining specter. GYRO!! I was level 12 for three years and once held the title of Commander Ganoush for 10 months. SPINACH PITA!!! (sorry; I can't help myself) Please get back to me with best career for me. TABOULEE GANOUSH!! I am anxious to start supporting Geela, Tahini, Scott, Baby Kabobby, & Cousin Shwarmi. (he is lousy man living in fig carton in my backyard. His sock smells. Hey, what's out there?) Can you help? I NEED JOB!!

Please give me dignified career like I had in Tezrhan. I was Commander Major in Army there commanding 16,000 mens in food industry. (Many listened; 2 bolted) FETA!!

Let's get me respectful career, Connie lady and Penn Foster Freeze school. I am more then ready.

College Graduate '020

Hamooli Kabobby

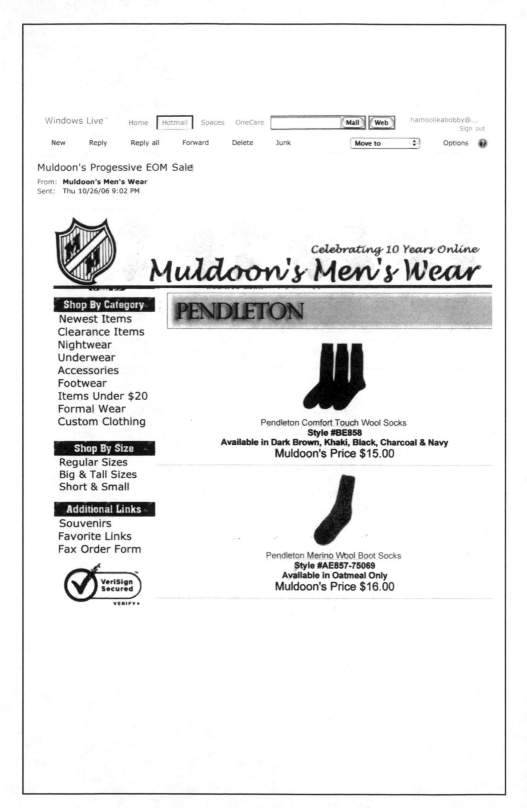

Muldoon's Progessive EOM Sale

From: **Muldoon's Men's Wear**
Sent: Thu 10/26/06 9:02 PM

Celebrating 10 Years Online

Muldoon's Men's Wear

PENDLETON

Shop By Category
Newest Items
Clearance Items
Nightwear
Underwear
Accessories
Footwear
Items Under $20
Formal Wear
Custom Clothing

Shop By Size
Regular Sizes
Big & Tall Sizes
Short & Small

Additional Links
Souvenirs
Favorite Links
Fax Order Form

VeriSign
Secured
VERIFY ▸

Pendleton Comfort Touch Wool Socks
Style #BE858
Available in Dark Brown, Khaki, Black, Charcoal & Navy
Muldoon's Price $15.00

Pendleton Merino Wool Boot Socks
Style #AE857-75069
Available in Oatmeal Only
Muldoon's Price $16.00

HAMOOLI KABOBBY
1413 1/2 Kenneth Rd.
#193
Glendale, CA 91201

MULDOON'S MENS WEAR
1506 So. Hastings Way
Eau Claire, WI 54701-4463

Dear Muldoon's Mens Wear.

Yes I am interested in socks. I like the Pendelton Comfort Touch Wool Sock. Size 15 ½. How do I get?

Sincerely,

Hamooli Kabobby

Hamooli Kabobby

Muldoon's MEN'S WEAR   EAU CLAIRE,
1506 S. HASTINGS WAY

Since 1950

Pendleton only makes regular size socks (shoe sz 6½-12) however, they have lycra in them & do stretch quite a bit
Thanks for inquiring

HAMOOLI KABOBBY
1413 1/2 Kenneth Rd.
#193
Glendale, CA 91201

Customer Svc
MULDOON'S MENS WEAR
1506 So. Hastings Way
Eau Claire, WI 54701-4463

Dear Muldoon's Mens Wear.

How can I stretch a size 6 1/2 sock to a size 15 shoe? Huh? Can
this be done? Toe will be squished. Feet hurt now. I like
lycra. (always have)

Do you have big mans gloves? When can I receive big mans clothes
when i order? How do i order?

Your company is highly recommended. Excuse language, I am foreign
but need big clothes. Thank you for help.

Sincerely,

Hamooli Kabobby

Don't know of any way to stretch socks. We have king size socks that fit up to size 16 shoe. You can access our website at muldoons.com + order online or call us at 800 942 0783 + order that way.

OON'S MEN'S WEAR

1506 S. HASTINGS WAY   EAU CLAIRE, WI 54701

Since 1950

EAU CLAIRE WI 547

30 JUL 2007 PM 11

USA First Class

Hamooli Kabobby
1413 1/2 Kenneth Rd #193
Glendale, CA 91201

91201+1421

PENN FOSTER
CAREER SCHOOL

925 Oak Street
Scranton, PA 18515
Tel 1-800-228-0799
Fax (570) 961-4030

**The U. S. Department of Labor states that <u>new job openings</u>
for professional Pet Groomers <u>will grow more than 22%</u>
during the decade between 2002 and 2012.***

Dear Friend,

Right now...all around the country...successful men and women are earning
generous paychecks in a career that is in demand. Many work for salons, kennels,
pet stores, pet supply chains, and veterinary clinics. Others operate their own
business. And all experience the satisfaction that comes from doing a job they love.   *huh?*

Who are these people? They are professional **Pet Groomers**...and you can join them
by earning your Career Diploma **in as little as six months.**

With Penn Foster Career School, you can train to be a professional Pet Groomer
at home, in your spare time, and **at your own pace.** There has never been a
better way — or a better time — to get the education you need for a career that is
financially rewarding and personally satisfying.

Enjoy a Complete Learning Experience
— for One, All-Inclusive, Low Price

Learn Valuable Skills on Your Time

The Penn Foster **Pet Groomer** Program was designed by experienced professionals
to teach the important fundamentals, the necessary grooming skills, and the best pet
handling techniques. Your courses include:

huh again ?

- Basic Cuts and Grooming Procedures
- Grooming Dogs with Behavior Problems
- Types and Personalities of Major Breeds
- Anatomy and Health Care of Dogs and Cats
- Equipment Use and Care

Sincerely,

Connie

Chief Academic Officer

HAMOOLI KABOBBY
1413 1/2 Kenneth Rd.
#193
Glendale, CA 91201

Miss Connie
PENN FOSTER CAREER SCHOOL
926 Oak St.
Scranton, PA 18515

Miss Connie & Penn Foster Freeze Career School:

I spill out my gut to you, my soul, my being, for dignified job
and you want me to be what? Pet Groomer? SALEELAMMM !!
HASSEUM!! I put curse on all those that wear smock. My wife and
I are living under plastic wrap in our backyard!!! That is our
situation!

In my country I was military detente leader commanding over
300,000 mathematicians in food industry dealing with high
government officials & ketchup. (sometimes mustard; brown) I was
responsible for the Moon Program in getting a Bazzarian to the
moon in a clean shirt. And you want me to do what? Clip and wash
dogs? Bathe cats? Scrape up hamster poop and turtle pellets
(poop)? I curse all small animals and the waste inside them. I
WILL NOT SCRAPE HAMSTER DUNG!

Sadly I must take this position. When do I start? EGGPLANT LAMB!
Who do I report to? When will I get paid? I will be pet groomer
and approach it with dignity & self respect. I will be happy to
pet wash and groom any kind of pet you have, Connie person of
Penn Foster Career Schools. I have goat in backyard that has
swollen teats now. (all 8) You know there's old Armenian proverb
that says: It is easier to admire hard work if you don't do it.
LARRY! My goat just grunted. It has something in its teeth.
What?

Please reply and tell me how we get me into program regarding my
new career at Sean Penn Freeze School. Enough with the military
commanding, Who needs it?

All Respect,

Comm. Hamooli Kabobby
Comm. Hamooli Kabobby

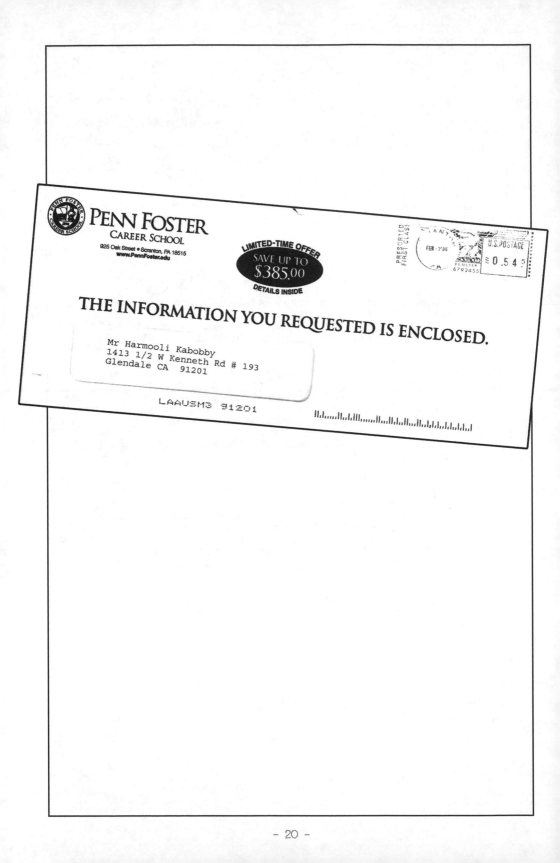

PENN FOSTER
CAREER SCHOOL
925 Oak Street • Scranton, PA 18515
www.PennFoster.edu

LIMITED-TIME OFFER
SAVE UP TO
$385.00
DETAILS INSIDE

PRESORTED
FIRST CLASS

FEB -3'06

U.S. POSTAGE
≈ 0.54⁵

PB METER
6792455

THE INFORMATION YOU REQUESTED IS ENCLOSED.

Mr Harmooli Kabobby
1413 1/2 W Kenneth Rd # 193
Glendale CA   91201

LAAUSM3 91201

PENN FOSTER COLLEGE

Thank You

Dear Hamooli,

I Am pet groomer (HW)

Thank you for your interest in our **HOSPITALITY MANAGEMENT SEMESTER ONE** program.

The information you requested will be sent to you shortly. Or you can go to **www.PennFosterCollege.edu** and find all the program and tuition information you need to make an informed decision today.

If you prefer, you can **enroll online** and begin your studies immediately.

Whether you choose to enroll via the internet, by phone, or by mail, you will receive all your textbooks, lessons, and supplies by mail after your application is processed.

Thank you again for your interest and we look forward to you joining the Penn Foster **HOSPITALITY MANAGEMENT SEMESTER ONE** program.

Sincerely,

Richard W. Ferrin, Ph.D.
President Penn Foster College

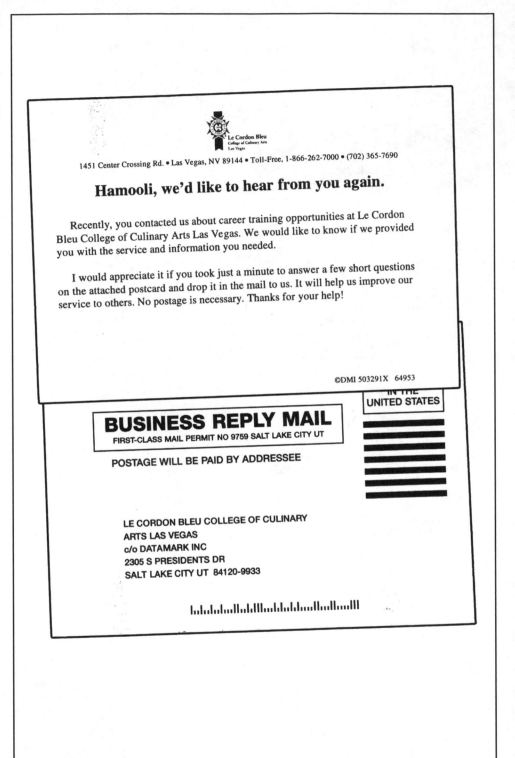

Le Cordon Bleu
College of Culinary Arts
Las Vegas

1451 Center Crossing Rd. • Las Vegas, NV 89144 • Toll-Free, 1-866-262-7000 • (702) 365-7690

Hamooli, we'd like to hear from you again.

Recently, you contacted us about career training opportunities at Le Cordon Bleu College of Culinary Arts Las Vegas. We would like to know if we provided you with the service and information you needed.

I would appreciate it if you took just a minute to answer a few short questions on the attached postcard and drop it in the mail to us. It will help us improve our service to others. No postage is necessary. Thanks for your help!

©DMI 503291X 64953

IN THE
UNITED STATES

BUSINESS REPLY MAIL
FIRST-CLASS MAIL PERMIT NO 9759 SALT LAKE CITY UT

POSTAGE WILL BE PAID BY ADDRESSEE

LE CORDON BLEU COLLEGE OF CULINARY
ARTS LAS VEGAS
c/o DATAMARK INC
2305 S PRESIDENTS DR
SALT LAKE CITY UT 84120-9933

HAMOOLI KABOBBY
1413 1/2 Kenneth Rd.
#193
Glendale, CA 91201

Mgt
LE CORDON BLEU COLLEGE OF CULINARY ARTS
c/o Datamark Inc.
2305 S Presidents Drive
Salt Lake City, Utah 84120-9933

Dear Cordon Blue College Of Culinary Arts & Mgt:

I need job now! I can cook! I have made following dishes:

GYRO!!
SPINACH PITA!!!
TABOULEE GANOUSH!!
EGGPLANT LAMB!
FETA!
LARRY!!

Let me explain my past employment history: In my country i was
pet groomer. I worked with dogs, cats, camels, hamsters and
turtles in high government position. I was military leader &
mathematician in Tezhran Pet Grooming industry. I commanded
32,000 pets under my command. (some almost ran off) I did
government accounting and was G-4 L7 Grade 19b organizer in pet
groom industry.

I did for 34 years, working with pets and around grooming in
accounting position. I have 24 years of mathematics specializing
in Yuro numbers in the spiff up specter. FALAFEL!! I was level
12 for over three years and once held the title of Larry for 10
months. I cleaned poop. Yes I can shave a mouse. Who do I
report to? When will I get paid?

You know there's old Armenian proverb that say: Man who wiggles
out of things needs teat reduction. I want this position! I will
not wiggle out of it. Hey, what time is it there in Utah? It is
9:00 here. Let's get me started!

Thank you,

Hamooli L. Kabobby

July 27, 2007

Dear Hamooli,
    I got your letter and am
very happy that you are interested
in our school! It sounds like you
are quite a cook. I would love
to get a chance to talk with you
about the school and your talents!
Please give me a call at your
earliest convenience and we can
talk about your future here at Le
Cordon Bleu College.

Le Cordon Bleu
College of Culinary Arts
Las Vegas

Le Cordon Bleu Colle...
1451 Center Crossin...
Las Vegas, NV 891...

07/27/...
Mailed From 89144
US POSTAGE

Hamooli Kabooby
1413 1/2 Kenneth Rd. #193
Glendale, C# 91201

1478

HAMOOLI KABOBBY
1413 1/2 Kenneth Rd.
#193
Glendale, CA 91201

Mgt
LE CORDON BLEU COLLEGE OF CULINARY ARTS
1451 Center Crossing Rd
Las Vegas, NV 89144

Dear Gordon Blue College Of Culinary Arts & Mgt:

Thank you for your short colorful note on expensive note
stationary. Your Note is now in box with other things i will keep
until they go in garage, then eventually thrown away.

Yes i can cook! I once made Feta Larry with spinach ganoush and
side of gyro for Grandfather Bahir and he got the trots. I have
wanted to do this since i can remember. Now it is done. Ha Ha
Ha! He run to side of building and squished.

I have no questions. Am i approved?

With respect for culinary cooking,

Hamooli Kabobby

Le Cordon Bleu
College of Culinary Arts
Las Vegas

July 27, 2007

Dear Hamooli,

You have expressed an interested in the Le Cordon Bleu College of Culinary Las Vegas Culinary Arts Program. You mentioned to me that this is what you have wanted to do since you can remember.

I am following up with you to see if this is still something that you are interested in pursuing. We have great connections to the Norwegian Cruise Lines and the famous Las Vegas Strip, so if that is something that sparks your interest then give me a call and we can get you registered.

If you have any questions or concerns please call me and I will address anything and everything. We do have several more starts this year; it is just a matter of figuring out which one is going to fit you best. I look forward to hearing from you!

Thank you

Le Cordon Bleu College of Culinary Las Vegas

HAMOOLI KABOBBY
1413 1/2 Kenneth Rd.
#193
Glendale, CA 91201

Mgt
LE GORDON BLEU COLLEGE OF CULINARY ARTS
1451 Center Crossing Rd
Las Vegas, NV 89144

Dear Gordon Jet Blue School Culinary Arts & Mgt:

Once again short note from me. I said "I wanted to give
grandfather Bahir trots since I can rememeber." And i did. he go
to bathroom on side of house many, many times in 48 hour period
from what i cook him. (Feta Larry with spinach ganoush and side
of gyro) That is what i said.

Am i approved?

With respect for culinary cooking,

Hamooli Kabobby

Le Cordon Bleu
College of Culinary Arts
Las Vegas

Dear Future Culinarian,

You have been Pre-Approved as a candidate for enrollment to, Le Cordon Bleu College of Culinary Arts, congratulations for taking this first step.

Our career oriented programs at Le Cordon Bleu College of Culinary Arts - Las Vegas, continue to be in high demand, we strongly urge all candidates to call toll-free (1-888-797-6222) within 48 hours of receipt of this notice. This will help ensure your application is processed and submitted to our acceptance committee for final review.

Once again, Congratulations!

Contact us today and learn more about **Le Cordon Bleu**.

HAMOOLI KABOBBY
1413 1/2 Kenneth Rd.
#193
Glendale, CA 91201

CREDIT LINE FOR U
Big Hip
888 Veterans Memorial Highway
Hauppauge, NY 11788

Dear You Got Cash.

I need to apply for your credit card. Where is it? I need it
now. How do I get it? (The $1500.00 - or whatever that is Feezi)

Thank you,

Hamooli Kabobby
Hamooli Kabobby

Feather*spring*

International Corporation
712 North 34th Street — Seattle, WA — 98103
www.featherspring.com — 800-628-4693

Special $50 Instant Rebate!

Dear Friend,

There will never be a better time for you to *End Your Foot Pain* with flexible Featherspring Foot Supports. The German manufacturer of the hand-crafted Featherspring Foot Support has offered us a substantial rebate on every Featherspring we sell for a limited time. So I have decided to pass it on to you to **End Your Foot Pain Forever!**

With this one time **Instant Rebate, your Flexible Featherspring** Foot Supports are at their lowest price in years. Because we guarantee to end your foot pain (or your money back), Feathersprings are a great value.

Now, with this rebate, that great value is $50 better!

Order Your Custom Formed Feathersprings today for Just $19.95 Down!

In order to take advantage of this special $50 Instant Manufacturer's Rebate You Must Order Now! At Featherspring, we have ALWAYS offered a Special Budget Plan so that everyone can get the Pain Relief they need and deserve. Just a $19.95 down payment (plus $5 for shipping and handling) is all you need to be on your way to pain free feet. Yes, you can pay the full price (after Instant Rebate) of $179.95 or use the Special Budget Plan of $19.95 down payment (plus $5 S&H) and 8 monthly payments of $20—No Finance Charge!

Full One Year Money Back Guarantee!

Of course, you will still have the complete Featherspring Guarantee of Satisfaction or your money back. You will have a full year to wear your custom formed Featherspring Foot Supports, and if you are not satisfied, just send them back for a full refund of the purchase price — NO QUESTIONS ASKED.

If you have been thinking about ending your foot pain, please do not delay because this Special Instant Rebate will expire in 10 days. Get your custom formed Flexible Featherspring Foot Supports for $50 off the regular retail price. Just send us your foot impressions today along with your order form, payment and the coupon below and if you prefer, you can even use your VISA or MasterCard — but ORDER TODAY!

To order, just fill out the order form enclosed in the Brochure and send the order form and this letter along with your foot imprint and payment in the enclosed Big White Postage Paid Envelope. You'll be glad you did!

Take Advantage of this Special Manufacturer's Rebate and Save $50

☐ FEATHERSPRING INTERNATIONAL BUDGET PLAN — I enclose $19.95 plus $5 (S&H) as down payment for delivery. I understand I will pay $20 each month for 8 months beginning 30 days after I receive my Featherspring Foot Supports.

☐ I enclose check or money order to Featherspring International for the full purchase price of $179.95 plus $5 shipping & handling.

☐ Please Charge my Credit Card (full information on enclosed order form)
This INSTANT REBATE offer only valid for the Next 10 Days

10 Times Larger (HL)

Mr. Foot President
FEATHERSPRING FOOT PL.
712 N. 34th St.
Seattle, WA 98103

Dear Mr. Foot President,

Listen to me. Can't think of foot pain now. Have problems - 3
family members living in 3 cartons in my backyard. Grandfather
Bahir is in refrigerator box. Scott live in a stereo carton after
his part of the umbrella collapsed. And the 2 girls, Tahini and
Maheeni share lettuce crate that is wet from ground. Geela & I
live under plastic wrap.

My loan with Armeniaquest fell through. By the way I am reference
#1696396. Coincidentally that is the rank of my own relative
Generalissimo Tazmak who we are very proud of in our small
country. He has many medals. Some he wears, others he just pokes
us with the pin.

There is no water in my backyard for shower! It smell here.
CAN'T WORRY ABOUT FOOT PAIN NOW!!! It is insult to all Bazarrians
with painful feet. HASSEYUMMM! I curse my toes!!!

But sadly I must have relief . for my foot. When can we work
together? I am ready? My shoe is tight as we speak. I just
bought a size 6 1/2 sock from Muldoons. I stretched it over my
size 15 1/2 foot. (It is lycra; which I like very much) What is
largest size foot support you have???

Shwarmi strings his underwear in his carton. He is pig with
bloated eyes. Hey, what time is it there in Seattle? It's 4 here
now. I have heard good things about Featherspring. (Some about
feet) People are cramped back here. Too close. Do my feet
smell? i ask you, mr. Foot President of Featherspring Foster Foot
School Of Feet. Here is my foot print as you ask for.

Respectfully,

Hamooli Kabobby

Jumping for joy — pain free!

Luxis International, Inc.
105 W Lincoln Hwy
DeKalb, IL 60115-8007

Phone: 1-800-628-4693
Fax: 1-800-261-1164

02/23/2007
Acct # 008991797

Mr Harmooli Kabobby
1413 1/2 W Kenneth Rd # 193
Glendale CA 91201

Dear Mr. Kabobby,

      Thank you for your interest in our Featherspring foot supports. In response to the letter you sent us, the largest size we can accommodate is a Men's size 14. For our Luxis Insoles and Footcradles the largest size is a Men's size 13. If you have any further questions, please write us or call us at 1-800-628-4693, Monday through Friday, Central Standard Time.

                         Sincerely,
                         Customer Service
                         Luxis International

```
                                        HAMOOLI KABOBBY
                                        1413 1/2 Kenneth Rd.
                                        #193
                                        Glendale, CA 91201




Customer Service
Luxis International
105 W Lincoln Hiway
Dekalb, IL 60115-8007


RE:  Featherspring Foot Supports



Hello Luxis International.

To my foot problem:  I compacted my foot down to size
6 1/2 through Muldoons Big & Tall Shoppe.  I did this through
their Lycra sock.

But I am afraid my foot will unfold inside your size 14 shoe &
flop open.  ANTONIO!!!  Hey, what time is it there in Dekalb?
It's 3 here now.

What can be done, Featherspring?  Where is my order?  I placed
order recently for size 22 supports and was told they are on the
way.  I have 1 Muldoon sock left and it is on my foot now.  My toe
is scrunched.  Let's work together to get:

A.)  My foot
B.)  Into your shoe


Respect,
```

Hamooli Kabobby

LUXIS
Jumping for joy — *pain-free!*

Luxis International, Inc
105 W Lincoln Hwy
PO Box 8007
DeKalb, IL 60115-8007

Phone: **(800) 628-4693**
8AM-5PM, Central Time
Fax: (800) 261-1164
www.Luxis.com

Mr Harmooli Kabobby
1413 1/2 W Kenneth Rd # 193
Glendale CA 91201

07/30/2007

Dear Mr Kabobby:

   Thank you for your interest in Luxis International products.
We received your letter in February of 2007 and your
letter of July 2007. The largest size we can accommodate for
our custom made Featherspring Foot Supports is Men's size 14.
The largest size we carry for our Luxis Leather Insoles and
our Footcradles is Men's size 13.

   In your recent letter, you mentioned that you recently placed
an order for the largest supports and were told that they were
on their way. We have not received an order at Luxis
International as of this date. If you have any further
questions, please contact our Customer Service Department.
Thank you!

                              Sincerely,

LUXIS
Jumping for joy — *pain-free!*
105 W. Lincoln Hwy.
P.O. Box 8007
DeKalb, IL 60115

Address Service Requested

UNITED STATES POSTAGE
$ 00.41⁰
MAILED FROM ZIP CODE

Mr Harmooli Kabobby
1413 1/2 W Kenneth Rd # 193
Glendale CA 91201

91201$1478 C008

BODY ODORS

msn Hotmail ▬▬▬   Today | Mail | Calendar | Contacts

⟲ Reply | ⟲ Reply All | ⤳ Forward | ✕ Delete | ⟋ Junk | ⤵ Put in Folder ▾ | ⎙ Print View | ⤼ Save Address

From :   <webmaster@badbreathexplained.com>   ↩ | ⌄ | ✕ | ⌐ Inbox
Sent :   Tuesday, September 26, 2006 11:25 PM

Subject :   Hamooli, this will help...

Hi Hamooli,

Have you tried desperately to get rid of your
bad breath?

— honn?

Let's face it, the truth is you are immediately
judged by the first impression that you make!

If you have bad breath, you will judged as an
unclean person whether it is your fault or not.

It's time to do something about it.

How would you like to be treated by someone who has
treated over 13,000 cases of bad breath?

These people paid upwards of $500 to see Dr. Harold
Katz, who is recognized as the leading authority on
eliminating bad breath

He is also the author of the "Bad Breath Bible" that
you may have already downloaded from our web site.

He has released his new complete Thera Breath system
that I am certain will eliminate your bad breath

I have been using Dr. Harold Katz's products for
years now and can't tell you how much it has helped
my own bad breath problem.

You have to see this incredible system yourself at:

Best wishes,

Webmaster
BadBreathExplained.com

Webmaster
BAD BREATH CLINIC
i Promote Media Inc.
15 Timberwolf Rd.
Brampton, Ontario, L6P 2B4 Canada

Dear Mr. Webmaster, Bad Breath Man:

Re: My bad breath. I am curious: Is this directed at my wife
Geela? I say this because she has in past punished me for my:
bad breath, foul body odor, stinky stretched out feet. But To be
honest: IT IS GEELA WHO HAS THIS BAD BREATH. Not me? Come to
Glendale and smell her under the plastic wrap and tell me what you
smell. I tell you truth. Excuse my English. I am foreign but
odor is odor. I want to be tactful here because Geela is still
flower but I am afraid bloom is crumple.

How can we work together to esponge Geela's foul breath? I CANNOT
SMELL THIS CAVITY ONE MORE MINUTE!!! Too close under plastic wrap
we currently live in!

I can not even grill back here. I recently bought very expensive
pig cooker and cannot grill on it. Too cramped, too many peoples.
I curse Shwarmi and his carton and his sock. My grandfather Bahir
is restless from all the peoples and the eyeing of everyone. He
has looked at my grill suspiciously.

I noticed you have treated 13 peoples with bad breath. I am
impressed. That is a lot. 13 anything is a lot. I once ate 13
hot dogs at contest and farted out a stream of noxious gas. Can
something be done with my wife of 27 years? Please tell me how I
can also get The Bad Breath Bible to read.

Someone is reading my mail! That's how I got into trouble with
Tammy. (Married lady who is no longer a friend.)

Respect me,

Hamooli Kabobby

⟲ Reply | ⟲ Reply All | ⇢ Forward | ✕ Delete | ⟋ Junk | ⬏ Put in Folder ▾ | ⎁ Print View | ⤵ Save Address

⤶ | ⟩ | ✕ | ⊿ Inbox

Sent :   Tuesday, October 3, 2006 9:28 PM

Subject :   Hamooli, it could be your tongue that is the problem...r

Hi Hamooli,

→ *hmmm ?*

Did you know that your tongue could be the root
of bad breath problems?

If you have a coat of white coloured paste on your
tongue, this is a breeding ground for smelly
bacteria.

We have added a new article to the web site titled
"Scrape Your Tongue" that will explain the benefits
of using a tongue scraper to remove this white coated
paste of you tongue.

You can read this article by going to:

http://clicks.aweber.com/z/ct/?dmfK7TYA93U_8kso8xd3PA

Best wishes,

Webmaster
BadBreathExplained.com

P.S. - It is very difficult to remove this white coat off
your tongue with just a toothbrush. Believe me, I've tried.

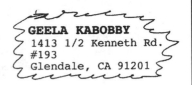

GEELA KABOBBY
1413 1/2 Kenneth Rd.
#193
Glendale, CA 91201

Websmaster
BAD BREATH CLINIC
i Promote Media Inc.
15 Timberwolf Rd.
Brampton, Ontario, L6P 2B4 Canada

Dear Mr. Websmaster, Bad Breath Man:

I am GEELA KABOBBY, WIFE of Hamooli Kabobby. I am MARRIED to this
man!! Let me say this at the start: It is Hamooli, not me who
has the bad breath. He is currently enrolling in Le Cordon Blue
Pet Wash Academy as pet washer and when he gets home from his day
he has foul breath. Not me, Mr. Websmaster. I once knew a
websmaster named Devon Shrang. Is that you?

Now down to <u>his</u> problem. Re: bad Breath. Hamooli has commented
to me that my tongue must be cause of <u>my</u> mouth odor. I say why?
he say that bacteria builds on the tongue and that he can not
approach me anymore. Approach me? Hah! How about I approach
him? (He not exactly hottie) He keep telling me to "Scrape Your
Tongue." Apparently he got this from you. Yes, he has a coat of
white coloured paste on his tongue. It is so thick he can barely
close his mouth. KAZEEEMAJ!   HALLESUMM!! I CURSE ALL COATED
TONGUES!!!

In our country an old wise proverb say: If camel walk for an hour
and does not reach its destination, then he is indeed sad camel
who just walked with coated tongue paste. I think this applies to
my husband.

Please, please, please. Someone keep an eye on grandfather Bahir.
He is restless. He has looked at Hamooli's grill.

Thank you for listening I know we can get something done about <u>his</u>
bad breath and white coated tongue, Devon Shrang. What time is it
there in Ontario, Canada now? It's 5 here.

Yours in good breath standing,

Geela Kabobby
Geela Kabobby

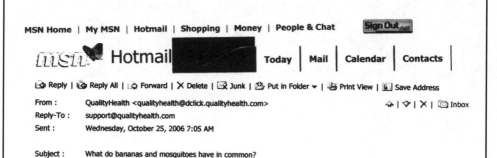

Today | Mail | Calendar | Contacts

Reply | Reply All | Forward | ✕ Delete | Junk | Put in Folder ▼ | Print View | Save Address

From :	QualityHealth <qualityhealth@dclick.qualityhealth.com>
Reply-To :	support@qualityhealth.com
Sent :	Wednesday, October 25, 2006 7:05 AM
Subject :	What do bananas and mosquitoes have in common?

⬆ | ⬇ | ✕ | Inbox

To ensure delivery of QualityHealth emails to your inbox (not bulk or junk folders), please add qualityhealth@dclick.qualityhealth.com to your e-mail address book.

QUALITY**HEALTH**.com
Your Healthy Lifestyle Resource

What do bananas and mosquitoes have in common?

What's the link between America's favorite fruit and summer's most annoying pest?

Click here!

Health Center: **Diet & Nutrition**

THE MORE WE LEARN ABOUT YOU, THE MORE **VALUE** WE CAN OFFER!

 Click here to see your top offer now!

The more questions you answer, the more offers you see!

Click here to answer more questions!

TODAY AT QUALITY**HEALTH** – YOUR HEALTHY LIFESTYLE RESOURCE

QUALITY HEALTH
BANANAS & MOSQUITOES PEOPLE
Marketing Technology Solutions
510 Thornall St. #130
Edison, NJ 08837

Dear Quality Health.Com Peoples,

I am BAHIR KABOBBY. GRANDFATHER to family. I am authorized to
read Hamooli's mail. (also look through sock drawer. Socks are
stretched to limit)

Now down to your question: I don't know. What do bananas and
mosquitoes have in common?

My answer would be one is long and yellow. And the other sucks
your arm.

What kind of question is that in the middle of all this?

HASSEAMMM KALABEEB!!! I CURSE ALL MOSQUITOES AND BANANAS!!

Tazmassian Respect,

Bahir Kabobby

Marketing Technology Solutions
3(C) Thornall St |||||||||||||||||||||||||||||||||||||
Suite 130
Edison, NJ 08837

Bahii Kabobby
1413 1/2 Kenneth Rd.
#193
Glendale, CA 91201

Bahir Kabobby
1413 1/2 Kenneth Rd.
#193
Glendale, CA 91201

February 21, 2007

Dear Bahir,

Thank you so much for writing QualityHealth.com and letting us know that you enjoy
taking our surveys. Since all of our surveys are located by going to our sites,
www.qualityhealth.com and www.nubella.com, and registering as a free member, your
study group members can do the same and we would welcome you sharing this with them.
We add new surveys frequently so please do visit our sites. We wish you a Healthy Year.

Regards,

Marketing Technology Solutions
510 Thornall Street, Suite 130
Edison, NJ 08837-2204

MTS consumer websites:
www.qualityhealth.com
www.nubella.com
www.healthpages.com

SHWARMI KABOBBY
1413 1/2 Kenneth Rd.
#193
Glendale, CA 91201

GEVALIA COFFEE
1102 3rd ave.   #501
Huntington, WV. 25701

Dear Coffee Peoples:

Who cares about coffee with all that's going on. I am COUSIN
SHWARMI and I live in fig box in filthy backyard. I wash out my
socks and underwear inside. It stinks back here. Too many
peoples too close together. I am part of family. I shower with
sprinkler and wash my yellow toes in Hamooli's drinking water. (I
curse his thick pock marked arms and discolored mole.)
HEESESHAMM!!

I know Grandfather Bahir is going to do something. There is no
electricity and he tries to plug in frayed extension cord into a
broken wall socket from patio next door. He wants to watch Judge
Joe Brown.   (he ruled against woman with rake on tv. she had
blonde hair)

How rich is flavor of your coffee? Is there no commitment or
cancellation fees? I am interested. What is your patented
roasting process? Tell me!!!

Respect from Feezi,

Shwarmi Kabobby

☾ GEVALIA®

Dear Coffee Lover;

Thank you for your recent inquiry.

We are pleased to send the information you requested and invite you to take advantage of our special introductory offer. Simply contact our customer service center to enroll today with a credit card, or complete the enclosed order form and return it to us with your prepayment. To expedite the ordering process, please ask our Customer Service Representative to locate your account using the address at which you received this enrollment form.

If you have any questions regarding our products or services, please contact our Customer Service Center at 1-800-GEVALIA (1-800-438-2542) 24 hours a day, 7 days a week; visit our website at www.gevalia.com ; or e-mail us at customer_service@gevalia.com. We will be happy to assist you.

Sincerely,

Gevalia®
Customer Service

☾ GEVALIA

Holmparken Square
P.O. Box 5275, Clifton, NJ 07015-5275

WWW.GEVALIA.COM

MAILER
$0.39
FEB 15 2007
US POSTAGE
FIRST CLASS
MAILED FROM 43123
011A0413004711

GL10 1320-4457   295
Shwarmi Kabobby
1413 1/2 Kenneth Rd.
#193
Glendale, CA 91201

01ABV

912013I1478 C008

SHWARMI KABOBBY
1413 1/2 Kenneth Rd.
#193
Glendale, CA 91201

GEVALIA COFFEE
PO Box 5275
Clifton, NJ 07015-5275

Dear Coffee Peoples:

Thank you for sending me more mail re: your coffee which i have
recommend to grandfather Bahir who drinks 10 cup day (he is very
jittery). Is there decaf for less jittery? He likes coffee but
should he drink that much? Gevalia is best coffee for him. He
poop a lot on side of wall. Bahir live in backyard and watch tv
mostly. He fool with frayed electrical cord all day plugging it
in broken outlets. He is madman. I am telling you, Gevalia.

I ask you: Is there no commitment or **cancellation fee** for signup
with you? I am interested. How much interest i dont know but
some interest. Like interest I have carrot cake. What is your
patented roasting process? Tell me!!! I NEED TO KNOW!! I am
roasting in hot backyard. Hamooli has discolored mole.

How do we get grandfather Bahir on your program of more coffee?
Thank you.

Respect from Jimke,

Shwarmi Kabobby

msn Hotmail   Today | Mail | Calendar | Contacts

Reply | Reply All | Forward | ✕ Delete | Junk | Put in Folder ▾ | Print View | Save Address

From :	Debt Consolidation Help <reply@scorescash.com>
Reply-To :	Debt Consolidation Help <reply@scorescash.com>
Sent :	Wednesday, October 18, 2006 9:01 AM
Subject :	Bling Bling for Your Bank Account

Get the dinero you need, fast. See here

PaydayHero.com, Inc
311 West Third Street, Suite 2292
Carson City, NV 89703
Remove Link

HAMOOLI KABOBBY
1413 1/2 Kenneth Rd.
#193
Glendale, CA 91201

PAYDAY HERO
211 West 3rd st. #2292
Carson City, NV 88703

Dear Pay Day Hero.

I need that $1500.00. Where is it? I want it now. How do i get?
How much is $1500. Feezi?)

Thank you,

Hamooli Kabobby (signature)
Hamooli Kabobby

msn Hotmail   Today | Mail | Calendar | Contacts

Reply | Reply All | Forward | ✕ Delete | Junk | Put in Folder ▾ | Print View | Save Address

From :	MyPoints BonusMail <BonusMailReply@mypoints.com>
Reply-To :	MyPoints BonusMail <BonusMailReply@mypoints.com>
Sent :	Friday, October 20, 2006 2:27 AM
Subject :	Order business and technology magazines and earn up to 150 Points

↩ | ♥ | ✕ | Inbox

To ensure your MyPoints email is delivered to your inbox, be sure to add **BonusMailReply@MyPoints.com** to your email address book or contact list.

MyPoints
Rewarding smart shoppers

BonusMail
Hamooli, your current account balance: 5 Points

Respond to offer and earn up to **150 Points**

Subscribing to business magazines made EASY.

- •Select up to 3 FREE magazines of your choice from hundreds of business and technology magazines.

- •No purchase necessary. No credit card required. No strings attached.

- •Simplified for you in one easy, single order process.

BAHIR KABOBBY
1413 1/2 Kenneth Rd.
#193
Glendale, CA 91201

FREE MAGAZINES
MY POINTS BONUS MAIL
188 Embarcadero - 5th Floor
San Francisco, CA 94105

Dear Free Magazines,

It's me, Bahir. Regarding your "Hundreds Of Magazines Free" mail
to Hamooli. (I peeked at his mail. Is that what he's doing with
all that's going on back here? ordering magazines?)

Who can think of magazines in middle of all this? Huh? It is
sweat box back here with all the peoples cramped up and the B.O.
It is unbearable. Maybe level 5. Or 6.

I can not think of magazine now. Or ever!!!! HASSEUMMM!! I
CURSE ALL MAGAZINES.

What kind of magazines? Any Turkish mountain bike magazines?
Send me. Make envelope to Bahir Kabobby. Not Hamooli!

I am looking for place to plug my electric cord in to watch Judge
Joe Brown. My sister in Meeziam say hello. She is taking swim
lesson and soon will swim better. (she wear rubber cap) She
swallow lot of water yesterday. her face turned blue and vein
popped. That fig Shawrmi laugh at her. I curse him under my
coated white tongue.

Respect from Heeshmayneea,

Bahir Kabobby
Bahir Kabobby

TAHINI KABOBBY
1413 1/2 Kenneth Rd.
#193
Glendale, CA 91201

CUSTOMER SERVICE
PAMPERS
Procter & Gamble
Two Procter & Gamble Plaza, TN-7
Cincinatti, OH 45202

Dear Pampers,

I am TAHINI, the oldest daughter in the Kabobby family (16; lived
in Glendale my whole life). Thank you for writing me. I didn't
know anybody knew I was here. Cool! I must tell you. BOTH
PARENTS SMELL! It is not just my dad Hamooli it is my mother
Geela who also has B.O. AND bad breath. They blame each other but
I have been in the same carton with them and it is like whew!
Stink-a-rino!!!   (Both have boils too.) I wish this was the only
problem.

Uncle Yaggi has come to stay in our backyard. He has fashioned a
makeshift hut out of the bubble wrap from the free umbrella and
lives in there. He has a man living in this bubble wrap with him
named Coco LaBoy. This man leaves the bubble wrap hut at night
with glitter on his eyelids and boyshorts and does not come home
until early in the morning with the glitter gone and mascara
running down his eyes. Dis-gus-ting!!! HELLO!   Pampers, what
can I do? He's a freak. I tell my dad Hamooli but all he does is
grill his lamb on his grill. (he loves that grill)

Coco works at that stupid "Barking Frog Restaurant." A frog
barks. How weird is that? They advertise free pudding skin on
Tuesdays. It is just a plaster frog that barks when you open the
door. Coco LaBoy has a strange red rash on his back thigh.
Pampers is the finest place to get Swaddlers from. I also am
interested in Splashers Swim Pants. I keep telling everyone that
Grandfather Bahir is going to go off. Soon. Listen to me!!!

And now this stupid Coco LaBoy is involved in our family. (Where
did he come from?!!!) Can I get an adult diaper for Grandfather
Bahir? He's gonna have an acc-i-dentttt. He weighs 200.

Stay Cool!

Tahini Kabobby

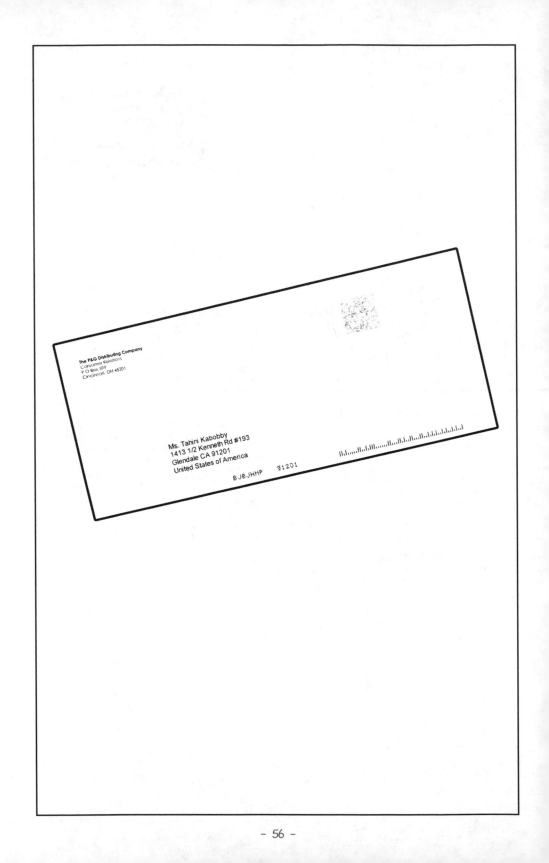

The P&G Distributing Company
Consumer Relations
P O Box 599
Cincinnati, OH 45201

Ms. Tahini Kabobby
1413 1/2 Kenneth Rd #193
Glendale CA 91201
United States of America

BJBJHHP   91201

The Procter & Gamble Distributing LLC
Consumer Relations
P.O. Box 599
Cincinnati, OH 45201
www.pg.com

Ref: 3038544
4/18/2007

Ms. Tahini Kabobby
1413 1/2 Kenneth Rd #193
Glendale CA 91201
United States of America

Dear Ms. Kabobby,

Thank you for taking the time to contact us. Our largest size diaper is our Pampers Cruiser size 7. The weight range is 41 pounds and over. We do not currently manufacture an adult diaper, but I will share your interest with the rest of the Team.

Thanks again for writing.

Sincerely,

P&G Consumer Relations
Customer Care Site C

~For office use only

msn **Hotmail**   Today | Mail | Calendar | Contacts |

⟲ Reply | ⟲ Reply All | ⇥ Forward | ✕ Delete | ✗ Junk | ✎ Put in Folder ▾ | ⎙ Print View | ⌄ Save Address

From :   Bexatrol <sales@healthyrightnow.com>   ↵ | ⟩ | ✕ | ⃞ KABOBBY | ⃞ Inbox
Reply-To :   sales@healthyrightnow.com
Sent :   Thursday, September 21, 2006 3:30 PM

Subject :   Still want to get rid of boils?

Hi Hamooli,

About Boils:

show to Geela

Boils are round, red, painful, pus-filled bumps on the skin that are caused by a
bacteria infection. When a staphylococcus aureus (staph) infection infects a
hair follicle it develops deep in the root of the follicle and works its way to
the skin's surface, forming a boil. Most people will notice mild pain, itching,
and swelling at first. Usually within a day the boil becomes red and begins to
fill with puss and becomes increasingly painful.

When a boil first begins to develop, it is small, red, and tender. After a few
days the boil begins to collect pus, which is actually a mass of white blood
cells that your body's immune system has sent to fight the infection. The center
of the boil begins to take on a whitish color.

Learning More:

Skin boils are very common and usually appear on the scalp, face, underarms or
buttocks. Although most people with boils are otherwise healthy, there can be
several reasons why you have developed a boil. Reasons your body was too weak to
fight the staph infection before it formed a boil include stress, illness,
decreased immunity, toxicity, allergy, poor nutrition, diabetes or thyroid
imbalance. Very rarely is a boil caused by poor hygiene. In fact, if you are
susceptible, you can develop a boil no matter how hygienic you may be.

Boils are exceptionally contagious. If the pus leaks from the boil it can spread
to nearby skin and cause more boils to form. Pus can also enter the blood stream
and spread the infection to other parts of the body. Multiple boils are called
carbuncles. Carbuncles, on top of being extremely painful, usually require
medical attention. This is why it is exceedingly important to heal a boil as
soon as it appears; not only will proper handling prevent a boil from spreading
or becoming worse, it can also help your body fight the infection quicker and
end your suffering faster.

 You have nothing to lose and everything to gain.

Call now for your risk free trial of Bexatrol? right now. It doesn't matter what
time it is we have operators standing by 24 hours per day seven days per week,
even on holidays to assist you toll free at 1-800-425-7005

To revisit our site, you can logon anytime to http://www.Bexatrol.com.

HAMOOLI KABOBBY
1413 1/2 Kenneth Rd.
#193
Glendale, CA 91201

BEXATROL BOIL PEOPLES
P.O. Box 1327
Cordova, TN 38088

Dear Bexatrol Boils Peoples.

I have your email about BOILS. It was sent to me. But it is not me who has boils. It is wife, Geela! She is loaded up with boils: round red painful pus-filled bumps. just like in your email. She has them on her buttocks. (like you said). Come to Glendale and see for yourself. (look at her buttocks)

Geela currently using combination of mop flog, Aqua Velva After Shave, and sponge peep but that just mask her boils. SOMEONE IS READING MY MAIL!!! I BELIEVE IT IS THAT DAMN COCO LABOY!!! He creeps me out. He is with Yaggi now. What are they doing in that bubble wrap from umbrella? I cannot even think about it. Yaggi is a mess too.

Did you know Aqua Velva also can be used to put on face after shave? Let me tell you an old Kaznazzian proverb: It is the camel with the large round red painful pus-filled bumps on its buttocks who has the discomfort not the other way around. Fartacus, 900 B.C. He is also author of book "Boils For Any Occasion."

Back to Botisol. Where can I get? (for Geela) Yes I have rectal finch! That, I think, is on a need to know basis. But it is not the carbuncles that she has. I use wipettes.

Please help us with Botisol. We are anxious. It is now 2 o'clock here in Glendale. I just had Marie Callender potpie. I think Grandfather Bahir has settled down. But who really knows with a madman like that. he has eyed my grill.

Respectfully,

Hamooli Kabobby

MACY'S UNDERWEAR DEPT.
P.O. Box 7888
San Francisco, CA 94120

Dear Macy's Underwear Dept.

I am Coco LaBoy and I am looking at your Macy's underwear ad now.
You mailed it to Hamooli Kabobby. But I grabbed it out of his
mailbox. Who is in that underwear? Is his name Kent? I am sure
I saw him at The Slop Bucket. I am delighted! How can I look at
more of your Macy's underwear products? Anything in fishnet?
What is this revolutionary moisture wicking cotton? Send it all
to me.

I am staying with a man named Yaggi in his umbrella bubble wrap in
this disheveled backyard of the Kabobby family. How crazy is
that?!!! There is another weird dude living back here named
Shwarmi that has his eye on me. I can feel it. Also the old man,
Bahir, is one crazy dude. He's getting edgy in his refrigerator
box and watches Hamooli grilling his food on his pig grill. I
don't like him.

I currently wear tiny socks with red "Wizard Of Oz" shoes. (2
inch heel) Some of the sparklies fell off but I don't care.
Everyone hates me in this backyard. I am the only person here
from the United States. I was born in Wisconsin. Everyone else
is from some weird country. It's a mess back here.

How about some more underwear mail? (Anymore with Kent?) What I
am living with back here is with bad B.O., foot smell, boils. I
am sick of these people. But I need a place to stay. Hamooli's
grandfather Bahir has not come out of his refrigerator carton in a
while. What is he doing in there? He is festering.

Sincerely,

Coco LaBoy

GRANDFATHER BAHIR SHOOTS UP A STARBUCKS

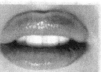

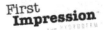 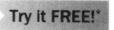

SHWARMI KABOBBY
1413 1/2 Kenneth Rd.
#193
Glendale, CA 91201

THIN LIPS PEOPLE
MICROSOFT CORP.
One Microsoft Way
Redmond, WA 98052

Dear Thin Lips People,

Listen to me. Hamooli grills all day with his barbeque pig
cooker. The smell is very, very bad. (That is 2 verys). It is
cramped mess in backyard.

There are 4 family members living in 3 cartons in backyard.
Grandfather Bahir is in refrigerator box. Scott live in stereo
carton after his part of umbrella collapsed. (It went down like a
crepe banner) And the 2 girls Tahini and Maheeni share lettuce
crate that is wet from the ground. I, Shawrmi Kabobby, cousin,
live in box that i can not identify in what is becoming a shanty
town back here. PLUS, Uncle Yaggi live with Coco LaBoy in filthy
bubble wrap packing. What they are doing in there is their
business. I look away. (I peeked once and saw nasty)

And now to add to this Hamooli grills all day. This is a gas
grill he prepares HIS meals on. He does not share his food.
SHALEELAMM! HAZZEYAMMM! Grandfather Bahir stares at him with red
Polaroid eyes. Scott has hair all over his back. He is like
wolfman when he turns around. I cannot look. (I peeked once and
saw disgusting)

Now down to your Thin Lips System. of course I am interested.
Who wouldn't be? Huh? My lips are thin!!! I would like to puff
them up like bolognas . Can this be done? Let me know. I have
been thinking about this. It is miserable back here. There are
mosquitoes (and bananas) everywhere.

Sincerely,

Shwarmi Kabobby

msn Hotmail   Today | Mail | Calendar | Contacts

MSN FEATURED OFFERS

COUPONS

SHWARMI KABOBBY
1413 1/2 Kenneth Rd.
#193
Glendale, CA 91201

QUIZNOS
MICROSOFT CORP.
One Microsoft Way
Redmond, WA 98052

Hello Quiznos!

I must be candid and upfront with you. Hamooli's grill continues
to be looked at with suspicious eye! This is serious problem.
This is grill he cooks on. Bahir eyes it. I know it! Bahir is a
nasty man with a streak in him.

Coco LaBoy is more disgusting every day. I wish he would move
from this backyard. he is not family member and disgraces Yaggi
with his sashaying and flaunting of his midriff & tiny socks. And
Wizard Of Oz shoes. I know he reads Hamooli's mail. I saw him
with Macy's ad that he took behind sprinkler wall. He is sad man.

Now down to your offer of free small Pepsi and bag of chips.
(with the purchase of any regular or large sub) of course I am
interested. Who wouldn't be? What kind of sub? My lips have
recently been operated on and are very, very thick. That is 2
verys. They look like two thick bolognas. They are sore and
bulgy.

When can I get chips and Pepsi? I will let out a belch in honor
of Pepsi. This grill problem is a mess. Bahir is like steam
cooker ready to go off. I am warning everyone.

Sincerely,

Shwarmi Kabobby
Cousin

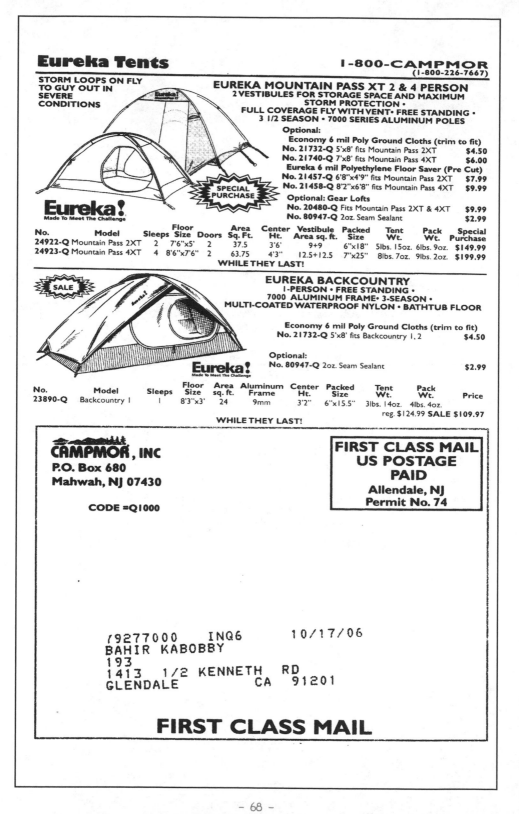

Eureka Tents

STORM LOOPS ON FLY TO GUY OUT IN SEVERE CONDITIONS

Eureka!
Made To Meet The Challenge

SPECIAL PURCHASE

EUREKA MOUNTAIN PASS XT 2 & 4 PERSON
2 VESTIBULES FOR STORAGE SPACE AND MAXIMUM STORM PROTECTION •
FULL COVERAGE FLY WITH VENT• FREE STANDING •
3 1/2 SEASON • 7000 SERIES ALUMINUM POLES

Optional:
Economy 6 mil Poly Ground Cloths (trim to fit)
No. 21732-Q 5'x8' fits Mountain Pass 2XT **$4.50**
No. 21740-Q 7'x8' fits Mountain Pass 4XT **$6.00**
Eureka 6 mil Polyethylene Floor Saver (Pre Cut)
No. 21457-Q 6'8"x4'9" fits Mountain Pass 2XT **$7.99**
No. 21458-Q 8'2"x6'8" fits Mountain Pass 4XT **$9.99**

Optional: Gear Lofts
No. 20480-Q Fits Mountain Pass 2XT & 4XT **$9.99**
No. 80947-Q 2oz. Seam Sealant **$2.99**

No.	Model	Sleeps	Floor Size	Doors	Area Sq. Ft.	Center Ht.	Vestibule Area sq. ft.	Packed Size	Tent Wt.	Pack Wt.	Special Purchase
24922-Q	Mountain Pass 2XT	2	7'6"x5'	2	37.5	3'6'	9+9	6"x18"	5lbs. 15oz.	6lbs. 9oz.	$149.99
24923-Q	Mountain Pass 4XT	4	8'6"x7'6"	2	63.75	4'3"	12.5+12.5	7"x25"	8lbs. 7oz.	9lbs. 2oz.	$199.99

WHILE THEY LAST!

SALE

EUREKA BACKCOUNTRY
1-PERSON • FREE STANDING •
7000 ALUMINUM FRAME• 3-SEASON •
MULTI-COATED WATERPROOF NYLON • BATHTUB FLOOR

Economy 6 mil Poly Ground Cloths (trim to fit)
No. 21732-Q 5'x8' fits Backcountry 1, 2 **$4.50**

Optional:
No. 80947-Q 2oz. Seam Sealant **$2.99**

Eureka!
Made To Meet The Challenge

No.	Model	Sleeps	Floor Size	Area sq. ft.	Aluminum Frame	Center Ht.	Packed Size	Tent Wt.	Pack Wt.	Price
23890-Q	Backcountry 1	1	8'3"x3'	24	9mm	3'2"	6"x15.5"	3lbs. 14oz.	4lbs. 4oz.	reg. $124.99 SALE $109.97

WHILE THEY LAST!

BAHIR KABOBBY
1413 1/2 Kenneth Rd.
#193
Glendale, CA 91201

EUREKA TENTS
CAMPMOR
P.O. Box 680
Mahwah, NJ 07430

Dear Campor Eureka Tents Peoples;

I need tent. I can't live like this much longer. Too cramped in here in wet carton that people see into. How do i get tent? I WILL NOT BE ACCUSED OF EYEING GRILL!!!

I have some dignity left. My socks are damp as we speak.

Thank you,

Bahir Kabobby
Bahir Kabobby

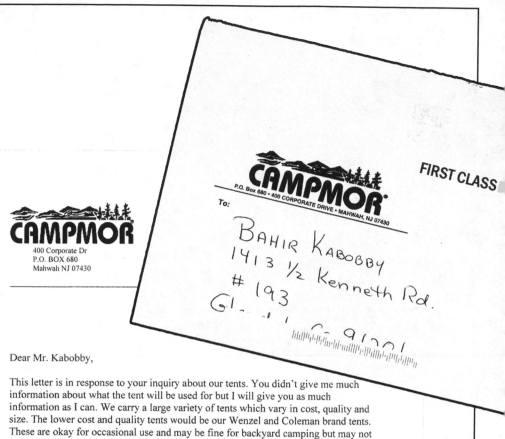

CAMPMOR

400 Corporate Dr
P.O. BOX 680
Mahwah NJ 07430

CAMPMOR

P.O. Box 680 · 400 CORPORATE DRIVE · MAHWAH, NJ 07430

To:

Bahir Kabobby
1413 ½ Kenneth Rd.
193
Gl.... ..... 9....

Dear Mr. Kabobby,

This letter is in response to your inquiry about our tents. You didn't give me much information about what the tent will be used for but I will give you as much information as I can. We carry a large variety of tents which vary in cost, quality and size. The lower cost and quality tents would be our Wenzel and Coleman brand tents. These are okay for occasional use and may be fine for backyard camping but may not hold up for long periods of usage. The Eureka brand tents are probably our best sellers and are good quality for what any family might need. They are a bit more expensive than the other two brands I mentioned but would give you many years of comfort in the outdoors. I am enclosing a copy of our summer catalog which has pictures of the various tents we carry. We also have a web site at www.campmor.com and you can see the pictures of all of our tents in color. Once you look them over feel free to call us to ask any questions you might have. Thank you for your interest in our company and I hope to be of service in the future.

Sincerely,

Campmor Customer Service

WWW.CAMPMOR.COM

BAHIR KABOBBY
1413 1/2 Kenneth Rd.
#193
Glendale, CA 91201

EUREKA TENTS
CAMPMOR
P.O. Box 680
Mahwah, NJ 07430

Dear Campor Eureka Tents Peoples;

Thank you for reply. I need tent. For 12 peoples in backyard.
Does tent have different compartments so we can all have privacy?
It is cramped back here. Money is not problem. Want best
covering. Tired of box. Need tent for myself and others who need
to come out of cartons. You have been recommend as THE tent
peoples. Can someones set up tent? I do not have grill! Hamooli
knows that.

Thank you, Campmor, for being quality company and helping others
with their covering problem. When can we take delivery on many,
many tents or one big tents?

Respectfully,

Bahir Kabobby

Cosmetic Plastic Surgical Center - San Dimas, California
Tel. 1-800- 816-0235

Dear Scott Kabobby,

Thank you for inquiring about our Cosmetic Procedures. You indicated an interest in:

- Hair Replacement
- Gynecomastia

Some information about the services you inquired about can be found at:

- http://www.cosmetic-plastic-surgical-center.com/foreheadlift.html
- http://www.cosmetic-plastic-surgical-center.com/gynecomastia.html

Financing/Payment Options: San Dimas Surgical Center has direct contacts with affordable financing companies. We want to bring our services within your reach.

The San Dimas Surgical Center strives to be the surgical center of choice for patients from all over the United States as well as from other countries. We are dedicated to providing the utmost in care.

Millions of people just like you, have turned to surgery to help create the total body they have always dreamed of.

Some men have significantly larger breasts than the "average" male. The term for this rather common condition is Gynecomastia, affecting a significant percentage of men. Although there are some medical causes of gynecomastia, there is no known cause or associated medical condition in the vast majority of cases. In many cases, male breast enlargement is due to excess fat in the breast area rather than a unique medical cause. This term for this is pseudogynecomastia and is by far more common than true gynecomastia.

that's me Scott

Ouch!

You'll be swollen and bruised for awhile – in fact, you may at first wonder if there's been any improvement at all. To help reduce swelling, you'll probably be instructed to wear an elastic pressure garment continuously for a week or two, and for a few weeks longer at night. Although the worst of your swelling will disappear in the first few weeks, it may be three months or more before the complete final results of your surgery are apparent.

I will try to reach you today to provide you with additional information. You are more than welcome to contact me between 9am to 5pm at (800) 816-0235.

I look forward to speaking with you soon

Thank you,

Consultant

Fatty tissue can be removed by liposuction. A small, hollow tube is inserted through a tiny incision, leaving a nearly imperceptible scar.

GYNECOMASTIA

MALE BREAST REDUCTION

toned
self-esteem
sculpted
natural
muscular
confident
buffed

SCOTT KABOBBY
1413 1/2 Kenneth Rd.
#193
Glendale, CA 91201

Consultant
COSMETIC PLASTIC SURGICAL CENTER
221 N San Dimas Ave #200
San Dimas, CA 91773

Hello Surgery Consultant,

I am SCOTT KABOBBY. Only son of Hamooli and Geela Kabobby. I
need hair replacement and Gynecomastia - male breast reduction. I
am 5 feet 2 inches and have a size 36 D cup male breasts. They
flop around when I walk up a trail. Sometimes men ask me out in
bars thinking I am a woman. From a distance I can look like Katie
Holmes. (But only from a distance) Up close I just look like a
short man with big yammers and a maroon face.

Lets get the hair and breasts done all at once. (Then we'll work
on the other half of the body: mole, hair, skin tags, new lung.)
Things are a mess here at home in the backyard so I don't need
this too.

Bahir is ready to go off. We can all feel it. Coco LaBoy has
told me this. People do not like Coco LaBoy back here. he is not
part of our family. They think he's a troublemaker. And Shwarmi
is trying to get him to leave Yaggi's carton and stay with him.
Coco Laboy is common street trash. But he dressed me up like
Katie Holmes once and I passed at a food court. (some hair showed
on my back) Thank you. I look like a melon.

Sincerely,

Scott Kabobby

what should I expect from
SURGERY?

Surgery is performed in our office-based surgery center under a light anesthetic. The surgery center is a fully accredited facility in which our experienced anesthetists have safely and successfully performed over 19,000 anesthetics since it opened in 1985.

The procedure takes about 1 1/2 hours and is followed by a brief stay in the recovery room before you are sent home with a friend or family member who will need to spend the first night with you. Patients from out of town may wish to take advantage of the services of a nurse or of a recovery center for their first night after surgery. Usually there is remarkably little discomfort after surgery which is easily controlled with mild pain medication.

The patient is seen the following day, small drains removed, and then sent home, frequently driving themselves.

Showering is permitted at this time and any type of clothing may be worn afterwards. A small compression wrap is worn about the chest for the 1st month to encourage the skin to shrink and to minimize swelling/bruising. Most men resume desk work within a day or two and start to work out again within two weeks.

Although the appearance of one's chest improves for several months after surgery as the last traces of swelling disappear, most men are delighted with their improved appearance on the first day after surgery. Unless there is an ongoing underlying cause for the gynecomastia, the results of the surgery should be permanent. Rarely there may be the need for a touch-up operation after one year, usually under local anesthesia.

how is the
SURGERY DONE?

The surgical procedure is tailored to the needs of the individual. Many men have excess fat over the chest as well as excess breast tissue.

Fatty tissue can be removed by liposuction. A small, hollow tube is inserted through a tiny incision, leaving a nearly imperceptible scar.

From : <client@cosmetic-plastic-surgical-center.com>
Sent : Thursday, October 26, 2006 1:44 PM

Subject : Information requested about procedures

Hello Scott Kabobby,

We have recieved your letter requesting information on the
two procedures hair replacement, and gynocamastia. At
this time we are not providing hair replacement but, we
are looking into this for future clients.

We can provide you with a free consultation so that the
doctor can evaluate you.

Please provide us with some contact information so we may
reach you. If you could e-mail us back with a phone
number or you may reach us at 1(800) 816-0235.

Thank You

The San Dimas Surgical Center

```
                                        BAHIR KABOBBY
                                        1413 1/2 Kenneth Rd.
                                        #193
                                        Glendale, CA 91201




BEST BURGER QUIZ
MYINSDIER DEALS
244 Madison Ave.   #238
NY, NY 10016-2817



Dear Hamburger Peoples,

How do I know which burgers are better?

With what is going on you expect me to give a flying pita?   Huh?

SASHIYAMMM!!!!   HEELIOMMM!!!   I CURSE ALL BURGERS EVERYWHERE!

I am living in refrigerator carton.   I am accused of things!!!



Tazmassian Respect,
```

Bahir Kabobby

McDonald's USA, LLC
2111 McDonald's Drive
Oak Brook, IL 60523

(800) 244-6227

August 20, 2007

Mr. Bahir Kabobby
1413 1/2 W Kenneth Rd # 193
Glendale, CA 91201-1478

Dear Mr. Kabobby:

Thank you for your complimentary letter. We're delighted to learn that you enjoy eating at McDonald's.

Our Menu Management team works very hard to develop great-tasting, top-quality food products that meet the many tastes of the nearly 50 million people we serve each day. Our restaurant employees aim to serve you the hottest, freshest food, served quickly and with a smile, like only McDonald's can! It's nice to receive your comments and know our efforts are appreciated.

Again, Mr. Kabobby, thanks for contacting McDonald's. We look forward to serving you again soon under the Golden Arches.

Sincerely

McDonald's USA, LLC
McDonald's Plaza
2111 McDonald's Drive
Oak Brook, IL 60523

Mr. Bahir Kabobby
1413 1/2 W Kenneth Rd # 193
Glendale, CA 91201-1478

Dear Mr. Kabobby:

912013 1478 C008

August 20, 2007

Mr. Bahir Kabobby
1413 1/2 W Kenneth Rd
Glendale, CA 91201-1478

Dear Mr. Kabobby,

Thank you for taking the time to contact Burger King Corporation. As a valued consumer, your comments and observations are very important to us.

It is very rewarding to receive a compliment about your experience at our Burger King® restaurant. We strive for excellence throughout our system - in product quality, in service, and in cleanliness; and it gives us a feeling of accomplishment in each of these areas to receive a comment such as yours. A copy of your comments has been forwarded to the appropriate management team so that they too may be aware of your positive experience.

Thank you for bringing this matter to our attention. We greatly value information from our customers regarding their experiences at our restaurants. I hope your next visit will give us another opportunity to provide you with an enjoyable dining experience.

Sincerely,

BURGER KING BRANDS, INC.
a subsidiary of BURGER KING CORPORATION
5505 Blue Lagoon Drive • Miami, Florida 33126

$ 00.31

Mr. Bahir Kabobby
1413 1/2 W Kenneth Rd
Glendale, CA 91201-1478

C℀UPSS1 91201

BURGER KING BRANDS, INC.
a subsidiary of BURGER KING CORPORATION
5505 Blue Lagoon Drive, Miami, Florida 33126 • (305) 378-3535 • Fax (305) 378-7462

COCO LaBOY c/o
HAMOOLI KABOBBY
1413 1/2 Kenneth Rd.
#193
Glendale, CA 91201

MACY'S UNDERWEAR DEPT.
P.O. Box 7888
San Francisco, CA 94120

Dear Macy's Underwear Dept.

I am looking at your Macy's underwear ad now. You mailed it to
Hamooli Kabobby. But I grabbed it out of his mailbox. Who is in
that underwear? Is his name Ricardo? I am sure I saw him at The
Man Hole. How can I get on your Macy's underwear list? I like a
flexible fit t shirt.

It's still a mess back here. I moved out of Yaggi's bubble wrap
and into Shwarmi's fig carton. He treats me better.

Bahir is ready to pop. I can feel it. He is moody and stays to
himself. The others accuse him of eying Hamooli's stupid grill.
Who cares about a grill. Puleeze. Bahir's getting edgy in his
refrigerator box and watches Hamooli grilling his food. I don't
like him. How about some more underwear mail?

Sincerely,

Coco LaBoy
Coco LaBoy

We haven't heard from you in a long time, Hamooli and we want to know what you are thinking (it'll help us serve our readers better in the future).

☐ I have decided not to renew my subscription to Good Old Days and here's why:

_____

_____

☐ I've just been busy so please DO renew my subscription to Good Old Days for one year (12 issues) and bill me later for $15.97. A savings of $19.91 off of the cover price.

1003106407290470199R0188891

Payment ➤

☐ Payment enclosed

☐ Bill me later

REMEMBER TO:

★ EXPAND YOUR HORIZONS!

Customer Number: 64072904701

Keycode: R018889

PLEASE LET US KNOW IF WE DISAPPOINTED YOU IN ANY WAY!

GOOD ⬩ OLD ⬩ DAYS

Dear Hamooli

   I'm the editor of *Good Old Days*. We work very hard every issue to bring you the very best stories. I hope you have enjoyed your subscription this past year.

   I'm concerned, however, that we haven't heard from you. Your subscription has expired and I really hate to lose you!

   There's still time to renew -- if you hurry! (And if you've decided not to renew, please let me know what we might have done better.) In any case, please reply using the form above. I look forward to hearing from you. Your thoughts about *Good Old Days* are very important to us. Thank you.

HAMOOLI KABOBBY
1413 1/2 Kenneth Rd.
#193
Glendale, CA 91201

Editor
GOOD OLD DAYS MAGAZINE
House Of White Birches
P.O. Box 9001
Big Sandy, TX 75755-9001

Hello, Editor, Good Old Days Magazine:

Just a short note to let you know - no, you have not disappointed
me in any way. (although others have) You say you have not heard
from me in long time and you want to know what I am thinking. I
am # 100310640729047019R0188891 on your mail. Generalissimo
Tazmak's military number.

I will not burden you with what is going on here. but suffice to
say - I long for good old days. In my country I had uncluttered
backyard. So thank you for asking about ME. Someone cares about
ME for change. (Not that infected goat of a man Bahir) It was
nice to hear from you. What happened? I was just thinking that.
This is what you might have done better: Nothing.

Let me tell you what is going on. I got my son Scott job at
Foster Freeze Penn Milkshake School to learn how to make
milkshakes. Well, he got a lot of strawberry powder on himself
and it won't wash off. The boy's face is reddish color with tiny
dark specks in it. His professor was livid. "How can you serve
customer with strawberry specked face?" he said. I shrugged.
It's just another BS problem. What with Scott's crap hair and big
tits on a man. What kind of son is this?

While I would like to say these are the good old days they are
not. Hey what's going on in Big Sandy, Texas? Huh? Bahir is a
sucked lime wedge of a man. I CURSE HIM AND HIS EYING MY
GRILL!!!!

Let's keep in touch. yes I would like in future to say you know
what those were good old days. How can we make this happen. I do
not smell, Big Sandy man! What's going on with my magazine? I'm
on a need to know basis. I saw bum sleeping under January issue
and thought of you.

Sincerely,

Hamooli L. Kabobby

LLSLL ✺ Hotmail   Today | Mail | Calendar | Contacts

🔔 Messenger: **Online** ▾

↩ Reply | ↩ Reply All | ↪ Forward | ✕ Delete | ☒ Junk | 🗃 Put in Folder ▾ | 🖶 Print View | 💾 Save Address

From :   Alibaba.com <tradealert@alibaba.com>
Sent :   Sunday, October 22, 2006 3:31 AM
Subject : Alibaba Trade Alerts - (Sat, Oct 21, 2006)

```
******************************************
Alibaba.com  Trade Alerts (Sat, Oct 21, 2006)
******************************************
Dear Bahir Kabobby,


Please find below the latest trade opportunities from Alibaba.


========================================
tents
========================================
NEW GOLDEN TRADE LEADS (Listing 2 of 16)

Sell Army Tent for 34 Persons  [China (Mainland)]
Product Name: Army Tent for 34 Persons
Model Number: 007-1
Place of Origin: China

Specification:
http://www.alibaba.com/trade/offer/detail/53034721.html?clicksrc=tl

Sell Washing Tent  [China (Mainland)]

The single type(2*2*2.3m)
Components:this equipment consists of gas cylinder, roof paulin, wind
http://www.alibaba.com/trade/offer/detail/53497256.html?clicksrc=tl

For an updated list, please visit:
http://www.alibaba.com/trade/search/1i1p2tyfchms/tents_.html?clicksrc=tl




================
USEFUL LINKS
================
Join Alibaba:
http://my.alibaba.com/trade/user/join?cd=0

Alibaba Help Center:
http://www.alibaba.com/trade/help/helpcenter?vd=0

Suggestion Box:
http://www.alibaba.com/trade/servlet/page/help/Comments
```

I need tent !
Bahir

BAHIR KABOBBY
1413 1/2 Kenneth Rd.
#193
Glendale, CA 91201

ALIBABA TENTS
SHANGHAI OFFICE
29/F, Zhao Feng Plaza
1027 Chang Ning Rd.
Shanghai 200050

Dear Alibaba Tents, Shanghai Office.

I write to you because I AM AT MY WITS END. I NEED A TENT!!! You
tell me of tent you have for 34 persons. That is what I want!
NOW! I am writing to Shanghai office instead of China office.
Why? Who knows? I also may be interested in washing tent you
mention in your mail to me. As i have socks and underwear that is
damp.

Hamooli's grill continues to be looked at with suspicious eye!
This is serious problem. This is grill he cooks lamb on. But it
is not me. Yes I glanced at it. Do i desire it? Yes. But i
will not steal Hamooli's grill. I CURSE HIS SHOWER THONGS!

Shwarmi refuses to let us near pile of whatever he has in his
bubble wrap home. Does he want grill? Who knows? Is he making
room in that pile. (????) When one does not let you near pile of
unidentifiable something, one can only suspect. YET I AM BLAMED.
WHO CAN TAKE IT?!!! WHAT IS GOING TO HAPPEN TO ME, ALIBABA
TENTS?!!!!

Please. I want to get away from this backyard. Soon. FYI: My
sister, Fasheema, is bad. She stopped taking swim lessons. She
almost drowned in 2 inches of water. She wears rubber cap that is
tight on her head. It gave her rash. My buttocks itch.

Sincerely,

Bahir Kabobby

DAMP
underwear

rubber
bathing cAp

Dear Bahir Kabobby,

Your requested product information is below. (Your keywords: tents

Sell Military Tent [China (Mainland)]

Features:
Material: 100% cotton canvas
Item: JXZP-A001
Fabric: Oxford cloth
punched felt inside
heat preservation
Fits 12 adults

New Companies

Jinjiang Xingtai Non-Woven Products Co., Ltd.

Wishing you every success in business!

Sincerely,

Alibaba.com

TAHINI KABOBBY
1413 1/2 Kenneth Rd. 193
Glendale, CA 91201

RACHEL RAY COOKBOOK COLLECTION
PMB 129
8601 W Cross Dr. F5
Littleton, CO 80123

Dear Rachel Ray

It's me, Tahini. Problemmm! I knew it was gonna happen. I tried
telling everyone: HELLO!!! We have a situation in the
backyard!!! Grandfather Bahir is nutz! Whack. HELLO AGAIN!! He
ran out of his tent and shot up a Starbucks. Put six holes in
their ceiling. Lots of shaken nerves! One guy stayed in line the
whole time and got his coffee. He kept his table by dragging it
in the line with his foot. People yelled it was not right to do
that.

My dad Hamooli tried to grab Grandfather Bahir. His eyes were
like Polaroids. He had drool coming from his mouth and infected
spittle. It sprayed off like a Boxer dog.

Bahir screamed in some gibberish language: I CURSE ALL FRAPAACINO
DRINKS WITH FOAM!" Many times I have heard him curse Starbucks
and their frappacino pumpkin drink. I like it! Cool. The dude
is bongo. Listen people!!! You can't keep blaming him that he is
eying dad's grill. I don't think anyone wants that old grill
anyway. Scott's skin is eroding. From some "treatment" he sent
away for. He looks very, very bad. His breasts are size 39
double d's and they hang like tassels. He looks bad in a bathing
suit.

When can I get my cookbook collection, Rachel Ray? You're tops.
I see you on TV all the time and I know you help people with their
problems. I am mostly interested in express lane meals. And
comfort food. I like custard. Thank you. Grandfather doesn't
have a sister named Fasheema and she doesn't take swim lessons.
Is anyone listening?

Sincerely,

Tahini Kabobby

HAMOOLI'S GRILL HAS BEEN STOLEN!

msn 🦋 Hotmail   Today | Mail | Calendar | Contacts

🧑 Messenger: **Online** ▾

📇 Reply | 📇 Reply All | 📇 Forward | ✕ Delete | 📇 Junk | 📇 Put in Folder ▾ | 📄 Print View | 📇 Save Address

From :	QualityHealth <qualityhealth@dclick.qualityhealth.com>
Reply-To :	support@qualityhealth.com
Sent :	Monday, November 13, 2006 7:06 AM
Subject :	Receive a sample of Bounce (r)

📤 | 📇 | ✕ | 📇 Inbox

If you are unable to see the message below, click here to view.

To ensure delivery of QualityHealth emails to your inbox (not bulk or junk folders), please add qualityhealth@dclick.qualityhealth.com to your e-mail address book

QUALITY**HEALTH**.com
Your Healthy Lifestyle Resource

Receive a FREE sample of Bounce® Fabric Softener

To keep your clothes soft and static-free, toss a sheet of Bounce into the dryer.

Click here!

Help keep your skin healthy and hydrated

Cold or dry weather can cause the skin to lose moisture fast, leaving it exposed to the elements and feeling itchy and uncomfortable. Treat your body right. Be sure to use lotion once or twice a day, particularly on areas often exposed to the elements like your hands, feet, and face. Take care to keep elbows and knees soft, and wearing loose-fitting, cotton clothing if your skin is irritated, to let it breathe and heal naturally.

» Tips on how to help prevent and heal dry, itchy skin
» Learn about substances that may irritate your skin

YAGGI KANOOSH
C/O KABOBBY
1413 1/2 Kenneth Rd.
#193
Glendale, CA 91201

BOUNCE
Market Technology Solutions
510 Thornall St #130
Edison, NJ 08837

Dear Bounce Fabric Softener.

I am YAGGI KANOOSH, cousin of Kabobby family. Yes, Bounce, I
would like to receive free sample of fabric softener. My brother
live in Afghaniran and is in electronics business. He sell
portable shoe buffer over there. He does well. You wouldn't
figure with all the dust and shmootz in Mideast that shoe buffer
would sell but almost every home has 17 of them. Yes I know about
all the sandals but he still sells them. (I always say he could
sell cold drinks to very thirsty people - he is that good).

When can I get my Bounce? I could use a Bounce right now as my
clothes are stiff. Hamooli's grill is missing. Did Bahir take
it? You, Bounce, decide. I can only tell you facts. But after
all eyes were on him he flipped out as you say in America and left
for that Starbucks. he is like rabid dog with Komodo dragon
spittle shaking off his mouth. (I was sprayed on way out)

I have socks and underwear that need softening. Can you soften my
socks and underwear??   a certain man friend of mine complain
about them. I can't tell you his name but i can give you his
initials. C LaB. he has been "cold" to me lately. I wait for
him at night but he return with feetzi marks on his face and
yahooees. What is going on, Bounce?

Regards & Respect for fabric fresh,

Yaggi Kanoosh
Yaggi Kanoosh

Hamooli Kabobby
1413 1/2 W Kenneth Rd # 193
Glendale CA 91201-1478

IndyMac Bank
Home Lending

Reference Number: 1696396

Dear Hamooli Kabobby:

Shopping for your home loan through Eleadz, Inc. is a wise decision. We hope you make another one by selecting IndyMac Bank for your home loan needs.

Compare Our Rates
IndyMac Bank is a direct lender, meaning no middlemen and no mark-ups. As a result, we offer some of the most competitive interest rates in the country. In fact, we guarantee to beat any legitimate written rate quote from another lender, or we will pay you $300*. And with our huge assortment of home loans, you'll find the loan that best fits your individual situation.

Special Offers & Guarantees
When you receive a quote from IndyMac Bank, it's as real as we can make it. Plus, when you deal with us:

- We guarantee to beat any legitimate written rate quote, or we will pay you $300*!
- Customers who apply online receive a $200 discount on our normal fees
- We guarantee to close your loan on time, or we will pay you $300*!

Next Steps
If we have not already done so, we will be contacting you by phone within 24 hours to review your information, complete your application and answer any questions you may have. If you need more immediate assistance or just want to contact us, call us toll-free at 1-877-603-4023. Please reference this number 1696396 when you call so we can review the information you have already provided.

You can also visit our website, www.indymacmortgage.com, if you'd like more information.

Thank you for considering IndyMac Bank. We look forward to helping you with your home loan needs.

Sincerely,

Vice President
IndyMac Bank Home Lending

Member
FDIC

EQUAL HOUSING
LENDER

HAMOOLI KABOBBY
1413 1/2 Kenneth Rd.
#193
Glendale, CA 91201

Garret Brief
INDYMAC BANK
7565 Irvine Center Dr.
Irvine, CA 92618-2930

Dear Mr. Briefs,

I am desperate. I need loan. NOW! I must gets my house put
together. It is very bad back here. My grill is gone. Who has
it? All eyes point to Grandfather Bahir. But he cannot be
questioned. Why? BECAUSE HE IS IN POLICE CUSTODY!!! He went
beserk at Starbucks on Kenneth Rd. Peoples ran out and police
came and took him away with twist tie cuffs.

Meanwhile i cannot find my grill. I will describe it to you: It
is metal with bars and briquette smudge on it. with 2 sturdy
legs.

My wife and I returned from Kashahali were we went on body
draining mission. We drained all fluids from our bodies and then
ate nothing but eggplant ravioli for 6 straight days. (Geela
pooped up a ravioli; i watched)

When we come back we find out: Bahir went goofy, grill gone, and
my son Scott with BIGGER breasts due to botched surgery. He now
has the breasts of a female baboon. His nipples are yellow. (AND
orange skin)

Now down to your offer. Let's talk poop ravioli as we say in my
world. Let's compare rates. Please get back to me with
comparable comparisons so I can make compared comparable decision.
With no middlemen.

Thank you, Mr. Brief man, and I look forward to hearing from you.
I am ready for info from Indymac. My house is pile of munched on
wood. There is still tiny gnawing going on inside the pile. I
hear it.

Respectfully,

Hamooli Kabobby

- 95 -

Make More Dreams Come True

Dear SHWARMA,

Kissimmee, Florida...Make More Dreams Come True™

Thank you for subscribing to the Kiss E-Gram, Kissimmee's monthly newsletter. With this subscription you'll receive periodic emails filled with useful travel information and special offers.

Plus, your complimentary *Book of Dreams* makes your travel planning easy and the accompanying *Kissimmee Vacation Values* gives you great discounts on lodging and activities...all to help you get "more" from your Central Florida getaway. Both should arrive in your mailbox within the next two weeks.

Can't wait to get started? Visit us at www.FloridaKiss.com. You'll find complete details for lodging...from quaint motels to luxury resorts, condos to cabins, villas to fully equipped vacation homes. Plus great activities, travel packages, and more!

Questions? You are welcome to call our Visitor Center Monday through Friday, 8 a.m. to 5 p.m. (Eastern Time) at 800-333-KISS (5477).

Kissimmee Convention & Visitors Bureau
1925 E. Irlo Bronson Memorial Hwy.
Kissimmee, FL 34744

SHWARMI KABOBBY
1413 1/2 Kenneth Rd.
#193
Glendale, CA 91201

KISSIMMEE CONVENTION & VISITORS BUREAU
1925 E Irlo Bronson Memorial Highway
Kissimmee, FL 34744

Dear Kissimmee Convention & Visits Bureau:

Whew. That is long address. There a lot of E's and M's in there.
(And many I's and S's.) I wonder if anyone misses an E or an M?
And calling it Kisssssseme. Or Kiiiisemmmmmee? I am sure of it.
What's going on with your name? There are other letters to use.

Now. My name is SHWARMI not SHWARMA. Shwarmi means the great and
wise and honorable man in Feezian. Shwarma is dried piece of meat
that rolls on spindle all day in Falafel restaurant. Do not
confuse the two. I AM NOT DRIED MEAT!!!

Now Let me tell you what is going on here, Kissimme, with Coco
LaBoy, my man friend. He has moved in with me. We both staying
in Bahir's tent while he is gone with Starbucks police. Coco has
left Yaggi's bubble wrap hovel and we live comfortably in tent big
enough for 34.

Who knows when that miserable Bahir will return. I know he has
that grill somewhere.

And now my daughter Asma has just told me her boyfriend was
flushed through Turkish sewer system. What should i tell her,
Kiissss-me?

So where do we stand?

Regards from Glendale,

Shwarmi Kabobby

SHWARMI KABOBBY
1413 1/2 Kenneth Rd.
#193
Glendale, CA 91201

KISSIMMEE CONVENTION & VISITORS BUREAU
1925 E Irlo Bronson Memorial Highway
Kissimmee, FL 34744

Dear Kissimmee Convention & Visits Bureau:

Thank you for replying to my letter to you. And once again you
address me as SHWARMA when YOU KNOW my name is SHWARMI!!!!
Shwarmi means the noble and proud wise person in Karzazzian while
Shwarma is crust that builds up in fold of armpit in Alabama.
Please: I AM NOT ALABAMA ARMPIT CRUST! (Do not confuse the two)

I need to tell Asma what to do about her boyfriend who was flushed
down Turkish sewer system and what do you send me???

YOUR BOOK OF DREAMS and you tell me to START PACKING. Packing
what??? In my country that is what you tell someone who insulted
you. Yes i am having dreams. bad dreams.

So...Kisssssssssiiiimmmmmeeee, once again I ask you: What should I
tell my daughter Asma to do about her boyfriend who was flushed
through Turkish sewer system? Do i tell him to start packing?
Huh?

Sincerely,

Shwarmi Kabobby

- 99 -

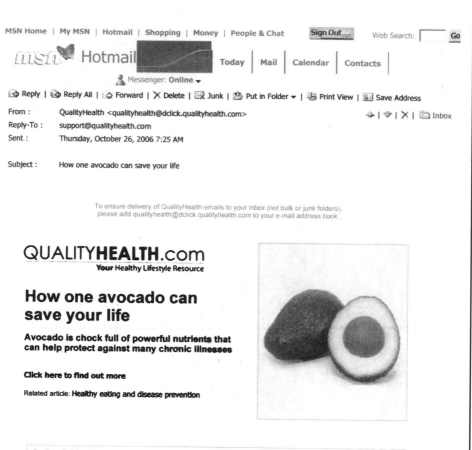

QUALITY**HEALTH**.com
Your Healthy Lifestyle Resource

How one avocado can save your life

Avocado is chock full of powerful nutrients that can help protect against many chronic illnesses

Click here to find out more

Related article: **Healthy eating and disease prevention**

THE MORE WE LEARN ABOUT YOU, THE MORE **VALUE** WE CAN OFFER!

 Click here to see your top offer now!

The more questions you answer, the more offers you see!

 Click here to answer more questions!

TAHINI KABOBBY
1413 1/2 Kenneth Rd.
#193
Glendale, CA 91201

AVOCADO SAVING PEOPLE
Marketing Technology Solutions
510 Thornall St. #130
Edison, NJ 08837

Dear Avocado Saving People:

A-Ma-Zinnnng! An avocado can save my life. Cool. How? I once
knew a girl in junior high school who's life was saved by a kiwi.
But an avocado? Incred-i-billll!

I am watching them now bring back Grandfather Bahir to the
backyard. The police are removing his handcuffs and my Dad
Hamooli is signing for him as we speak. Bahir's shirt is dirty.
Wheweee!

They are placing him back in his Refrigerator box which was
vacated when he left. (Coco & Shwarmi have his tent)

I will give him an avocado if it means saving his life. He is
still very, very angry. Hamooli's grill is missing.   I am doing
pretty good in school this years mostly a's and a few b's. But my
grades are up. Thanks, avocado people for being there for our
family. You are a life saver.

Tahini Kabobby

GEELA KABOBBY
1413 1/2 Kenneth Rd.
#193
Glendale, CA 91201

PENNY SAVER
Harte Hanks Shoppers
2830 Orbiter St. P.O. Box 8900
Brea, CA 92822-8900

Dear Penny Saver Coupon,

Re: Your carpet cleaning ad sent to me.

I have no hallway. I have no bedroom. I have no 2 rooms. I have
no upholstery. Why? BECAUSE I HAVE NO HOME!! The termites have
eaten my house! Down to floor. WE ARE LIVING IN CARDBOARD BOXES
IN BACKYARD!!!! Why do you send me carpet cleaning coupons? I
blame Hamooli for everyhting. He is like center of rotten figs.

However, I do have Oriental rug i want washed. Shwarmi and that
disgusting Coco LaBoy were on it. What they do on it is anybody's
business. i can only imagine. HALLELAMMI!

So sadly I need your service. To clean rug which is under bubble
wrap now. How much? Can you remove pet odor and deep clean a
pungency of spoonge? Who is that man in ad? What is that machine
in front of him?

How can we further our cleansing of this rug? I pray 57 times a
day now.

Respect for Oriental Carpet,

Geela Kabobby

Reply | Reply All | Forward | ✕ Delete | Junk | Put in Folder ▾ | Print View | Save Address

From :	Credit Line 4 U <replyto@chocolatepunche.com>
Reply-To :	Credit Line 4 U <replyto@chocolatepunche.com>
Sent :	Thursday, October 19, 2006 11:01 AM
Subject :	Instantly Use Your VueMasterCard

◆ | ▽ | ✕ | Inbox

If you are unable to view this important page, please refresh this page.
For Outlook users, if the below graphics are not viewable, right click on the image and select, 'Add Sender to Safe Senders List'.

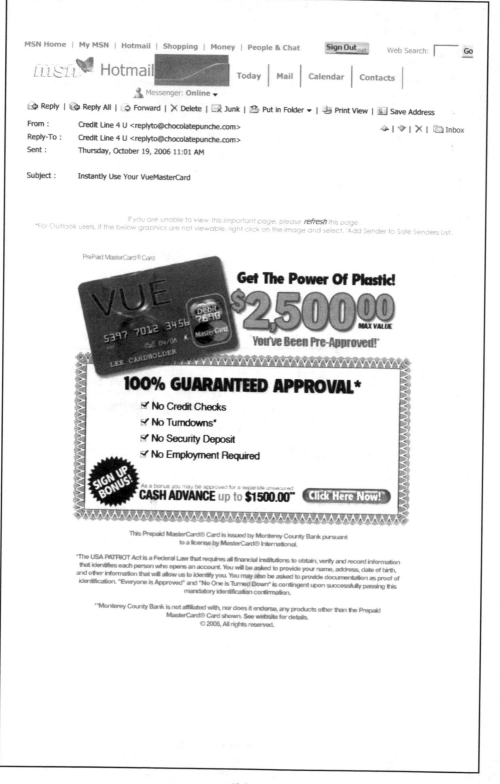

PrePaid MasterCard® Card

Get The Power Of Plastic!

VUE 5397 7012 3456 Debit 7690 MasterCard LEE CARDHOLDER

$2,500.00 MAX VALUE

You've Been Pre-Approved!

100% GUARANTEED APPROVAL*

☑ No Credit Checks
☑ No Turndowns*
☑ No Security Deposit
☑ No Employment Required

SIGN UP BONUS!

As a bonus you may be approved for a separate unsecured

CASH ADVANCE up to **$1500.00**   Click Here Now!

This Prepaid MasterCard® Card is issued by Monterey County Bank pursuant
to a license by MasterCard® International.

*The USA PATRIOT Act is a Federal Law that requires all financial institutions to obtain, verify and record information
that identifies each person who opens an account. You will be asked to provide your name, address, date of birth,
and other information that will allow us to identify you. You may also be asked to provide documentation as proof of
identification. "Everyone is Approved" and "No One is Turned Down" is contingent upon successfully passing this
mandatory identification confirmation.

**Monterey County Bank is not affiliated with, nor does it endorse, any products other than the Prepaid
MasterCard® Card shown. See website for details.
© 2006, All rights reserved.

HAMOOLI KABOBBY
1413 1/2 Kenneth Rd.
#193
Glendale, CA 91201

VUE CREDIT CARD
CREDIT LINE FOR U
Big Hip
888 Veterans Memorial Highway
Hauppauge, NY 11788   10/06

Dear Vue Credit Card.

Where is it? The cash. I need it now. How do I get it? (The
$2500.00 - or whatever that is Tazmati)

Thank you,

Hamooli Kabobby
Hamooli Kabobby

Holland America Line

A Signature of Excellence

Guest ID# 359059748

Hamooli Kabobby
1413 1/2 W Kenneth Rd # 193
Glendale CA 91201-1478
||I.|....||.||.|||I......||I..||.||.||...||.||.||.|.||.|.||.|

Dear Hamooli Kabobby,

Thank you for your interest in Alaska and the Yukon. Our comprehensive 2006 program of cruises and cruisetours is the most distinctive to date. With awesome glaciers, mountains, rivers, and wildlife plus extra, unscheduled time for intriguing wilderness activities, it's the best way to see and do it all.

To get the most out of your Great Land adventure, **take the time to fully experience the natural wonders of Alaska and the Yukon** on a 10- to 20-day cruisetour. All cruisetours feature leisurely glacier viewing aboard your five-star Holland America Line ship. With scenic travel deep into the heartland via luxury railcar and motorcoach and multi-day stays in legendary places like Denali National Park, you can truly connect with nature on land.

Seven-day cruises illuminate the glaciers and most popular ports of the Alaskan coastline. Take your pick of three different ways to cruise the Inside Passage and beyond. We feature appealing Holland America extras—Glacier Bay narration by a Park Ranger and a Huna Totem Native speaker and the best ports in Southeast Alaska including Juneau, Ketchikan, Sitka, Skagway, Haines and, **new for 2006**, Icy Strait Point.

- Choose from 8 ships sailing from Seattle, Vancouver and Seward.
- Cruises feature **select glacier viewing experiences**: Glacier Bay National Park, College Fjord, Tracy Arm or massive Hubbard Glacier.
- All cruises offer the dynamic insight of **onboard naturalists** and **Native Alaskan Artists in Residence** to underscore the richness and diversity of the places you'll be visiting.

Look no further for the ultimate Alaska vacation experience. Holland America Line offers more of the national parks in Alaska and the Yukon plus those highly personal adventures that add depth to your wilderness discovery. Whether you choose a cruise or a cruisetour, you'll experience the Alaska of your dreams.

Sincerely,

Sounds cold!
I need

Stein Kruse
President and Chief Executive Officer

```
                                          HAMOOLI KABOBBY
                                          1413 1/2 Kenneth Rd.
                                          #193
                                          Glendale, CA 91201
```

Stein Kruse
HOLLAND AMERICA CRUISE LINE
P.O. Box 34985
Seattle, WA 98124

Dear Mr. Stein Kruse, Holland Cruise Line,

Thank you for writing me with suggestion i cruise to Alaska. I am
ready! With all that's going on here in Glendale, I am anxious to
get to new environment. The cold and snow of Alaska will be good
for me. Open my nostrils, so to speak, and forget my problems.
With the dog sledding and mushing and glaciers it seems what I
should be doing. You talked me into it! When do I go? PRAISE
ALASKA! I am waiting for my $2500.00 from Vue Credit card to pay
for trip. I feel the cold now. I AM MORE THEN READY!!

Mr. Stein Kruse, funny how your last name, Kruse, is what you do,
send people on cruise. Interesting, that is now 2 peoples I have
met in my lifetimes with this happening. I knew man once in my
country who's name was Kajian L. Petgroomer and he was actually a
petgroomer. He smelled of Schnauzer hairs all the time. I wiffed
him as much as i could.

Now down to business: Let's talk testicles. It is time now to
get away. Without Geela. With all the talk of odor and bad
breath and boils who needs it? So yes I want to go to Alaska.
(Maybe Yukon too) when do we leave? When can i go to Dawson
City? I am ready. More ready then even a few sentences ago. I
may take 9 peoples with me. from backyard. Can we all stay in 1
room? Some in hallway????

So what's next? If you even have colder places than Alaska, bring
it on. I want to freeze. I need it

Respectfully,

Hamooli Kabobby

GEELA KABOBBY
1413 1/2 Kenneth Rd.
#193
Glendale, CA 91201

Stein Kruse
HOLLAND AMERICA CRUISE LINE
P.O. Box 34985
Seattle, WA 98124

Dear Mr. Stein Kruse, Holland Cruise Line,

YOU CAN NOT SEND HAMOOLI TO ALASKA! Hamooli knows he is not
allowed in Alaska due to medical, personal, & Alaskan reasons. He
can infect no one anymore. Every electronic bracelet on his body
will beep.

Listen to me: HIS GRILL HAS BEEN STOLEN! That is problem facing
us all now. Do you know, Mr. Stein Kruse, that Hamooli's sister
Feroozi looks just like Hamooli. Down to the hair in his
discolored mole. something is wrong here. In 1992 Feroozi was
quarantined with drip from her nostril. She has Harn's Drip. Her
nose has spoonge. I CAN'T TAKE IT! FEEZILAMMM! Who can look at
a dripping nose all day with feedge on it? Huh? Can you? I
don't think so. I now face the East and boil water. (For
Feroozi) Hamooli sent me picture of Feroozi with this drip on it.

The Alaskan peoples deserve better. Do not send him there!!!

Come up with somewhere else for Hamooli to go. He needs break
from backyard with the odor, cramped living, and grill gone.   And
now with Bahir returned to backyard it will only get worse.
Especially with grill stolen. His family is a mess. don't put
them all in 1 room. I beg you!!!

Respectfully,

Geela Kabobby

Holland America Line
A Signature of Excellence

February, 20th 2007

Dear Hamoobi,

Thank you for your interest in Holland America Line. We look forward to having you and your family onboard one fabulous destinations!

I am a Personal Cruise Consultant for Holland America Line. I have been assigned to assist you with any of your future cruising needs on Holland America Line.

Currently we have special promotion offerings to Alaska for 2007. Although we do not have family rates on our voyages, we do have special rates for third and fourth guests in one stateroom. The maximum occupancy in any of our staterooms is 4 guests.

Our Alaska season is currently 80% sold out, with most of our space available on our round trip Seattle sailings. There is limited space available on our CruiseTour packages (cruise and land options). Please see the enclosed brochure for more information on our cruise and tour offerings.

Alaska is our coldest destination, followed by the Baltic cruises in Europe.

Please feel free to contact me if you have any questions.

Kind Regards

```
                                        HAMOOLI KABOBBY
                                        1413 1/2 Kenneth Rd.
                                        #193
                                        Glendale, CA 91201
```

Cruise Specialist
HOLLAND AMERICA CRUISE LINE
P.O. Box 34985
Seattle, WA 98124

Dear Ms Cruise Specialist,

My name is Hamooli. Not Hamoobi. You addressed me as Hamoobi.
But thank you for writing me with Alaska cruise information.

Now down to cruise business. Forget what Geela say. I can go to
Alaska. There is no medical reason not to send me to Alaska.
(all shots complete, all charts initialed)

Yes, my grill has been stolen and i need to get away but Geela is
insulting to myself and my sister Feroozi (who does not look like
me. She look like reality star Moesha, if anything.)

We all need to go on cruise! Please let me know: If more then 4
in room can be waived.

There are many in our group. Holland Cruise is highly recommended
and 11 of us want to take Alaskan cruise. How can we arrange? We
are prepared to cruise 90 days or more. (In Alaska)

Respectfully,

Hamooli Kabobby

Hamooli Kabobby

Holland America Line

A Signature of Excellence

Dear Hamooli Kabobby,

Thank you for visiting www.hollandamerica.com.

We appreciate your interest in cruising with Holland America Line and hope that it inspires you to join us on one of our distinctive cruises. In the meantime, we invite you to return to www.hollandamerica.com to explore our nearly 500 cruises to all seven continents on 13 spacious ships.

While visiting www.hollandamerica.com, you can download brochures, access itineraries, and take virtual tours of our ships, luxurious accommodations, favorite destinations and more.

Thanks again for your interest, and we look forward to welcoming you aboard.

Kind Regards,

Holland America Line

GENERALISSIMO TAZMAK

HAS ARRIVED!

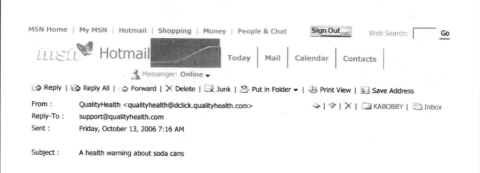

msn Hotmail   Today | Mail | Calendar | Contacts

Messenger: **Online** ▾

Reply | Reply All | Forward | ✕ Delete | Junk | Put in Folder ▾ | Print View | Save Address

From :	QualityHealth <qualityhealth@dclick.qualityhealth.com>
Reply-To :	support@qualityhealth.com
Sent :	Friday, October 13, 2006 7:16 AM

Subject :   A health warning about soda cans

To ensure delivery of QualityHealth emails to your inbox (not bulk or junk folders),
please add qualityhealth@dclick.qualityhealth.com to your e-mail address book.

QUALITY**HEALTH**.com
Your Healthy Lifestyle Resource

A health warning about soda cans

Drinking straight from soda cans can be dangerous to your health. Find out how to protect yourself.

Click here!

Health Center: **Diet & Nutrition**

THE MORE WE LEARN ABOUT YOU, THE MORE **VALUE** WE CAN OFFER!

  Click here to see your top offer now!

The more questions you answer, the more offers you see!

Click here to answer more questions!

TODAY AT QUALITY**HEALTH** – YOUR HEALTHY LIFESTYLE RESOURCE

SHWARMI KABOBBY
1413 1/2 Kenneth Rd.
#193
Glendale, CA 91201

SODA CANS PEOPLE
QUALITY HEALTH
510 Thornail St.
#130
Edison, NJ 08837

Dear Soda Cans Peoples:

I am avid reader of Quality Health.com. It is only .com I read.
Why can drinking straight from soda cans be dangerous to my
health? I do it all the time. I just had a Sprite. (straight
from can). Soon i will drink Pepsi. from can.

WHO CAN THINK OF SUCH DRIBBLE AT TIME LIKE THIS?????!
Generalissimo Tazmak has arrived in Kabobby backyard for full
military inspection.

His medals glistened off his uniform. he stood ramrod straight.
He is impressive military figure. Number 28761-BL. He is here to
find Hamooli's grill and interrogated everyone. He has come with
his aide Kajian Petgroomer.

And lined us all up in backyard: Hamooli, Geela, Tahini, Scott,
Baby Meheeni, Yaggi, Bahir, and Coco LaBoy. (Who is my friend)
Tazmak eyed us with glint. He will find grill. He cracked his
whip. Coco flinched. but he liked it. I could tell.

Tell me more about sodas from can. I just had Diet Mountain Dew
as i write this. (from can) I looked at my bologna thick lip.
It is normal.

Respect,

Shwarmi Kabobby

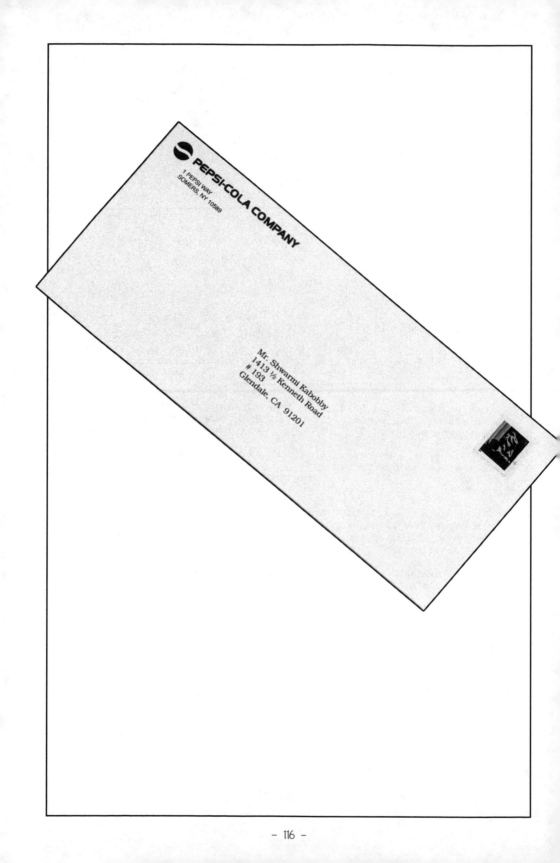

PEPSI-COLA COMPANY
1 PEPSI WAY
SOMERS, NY 10589

Mr. Shwarmi Kabobby
1413 ½ Kenneth Road
193
Glendale, CA 91201

PEPSI-COLA COMPANY

March 1, 2007

Mr. Shwarmi Kabobby
1413 ½ Kenneth Road
193
Glendale, CA 91201

Dear Mr. Kabobby:

Thank you for taking the time to write to us here at Pepsi-Cola Company. Your correspondence has just been forwarded to my attention with a request to personally respond. Please know that we always enjoy hearing from our consumers and consider this a real chance to communicate with you directly and address your concerns.

For over a century now, Pepsi has been producing some of the best-known and well-loved soft drinks on earth. Everyone here works very hard to ensure the quality, great taste and wholesomeness of our products. Each bottle and can that we produce follows stringent guidelines approved by the Food and Drug Administration (FDA). They are thoroughly checked by a Quality Control Manager and team.

We are at a loss to explain why anyone would pass along incorrect information to you about our containers. Of course, Pepsi-Cola Company would not make anything available to our consumers unless it meets the highest standards of excellence. Just as our consumers are devoted to us, we are devoted and dedicated to our patrons.

Again, we thank you for making us aware of the incorrect information given to you. We value you giving us this opportunity to address the subject and reassure you about our products and packaging. In that spirit, I have taken the liberty of enclosing something to remember your friends here at Pepsi. We hope your stay in our country is enjoyable and we feel fortunate to consider you one of our truly valued consumers. Always remember to "take care and have a Pepsi day"!

Sincerely,

Consumer Relations Representative

BRITE SMILE.

September 30, 2004

490 North Wiget Lane
Walnut Creek, CA 94598
TEL 925·941·6260   FAX 925·941·6266
www.britesmile.com

Hamooli Kabobby
1413 1/2 W Kenneth Rd
193
Glendale, CA 91201-1478

Dear Hamooli,

yes I Do!

Want to see how you could look with a whiter, healthier smile?

Now you can, instantly.

Call BriteSmile today and ask about the revolutionary Magic Mirror – it predicts what you will look like after a BriteSmile experience **before** having it done. There is no risk and no obligation. Call 1-888-227-1839 today.

When you do call and schedule an appointment you can **save $100**. We're confident you'll love your one hour BriteSmile teeth whitening treatment, and enjoy the remarkable results for years. Your satisfaction is guaranteed.

So call 1-888-227-1839 and mention priority code 0409-RNBL to receive your special savings. You can choose to have your priority appointment in the local BriteSmile Teeth Whitening Spa or a BriteSmile certified dentist near you. Offer expires October 21, so call now.

Look and be your best today,

President

P.S. When you call, ask about our special savings on BriteSmile gift certificates – a perfect idea for the Holidays.

Offer expires on October 21, 2004. Terms and conditions may apply. Call for details.

HAMOOLI KABOBBY
1413 1/2 Kenneth Rd.
#193
Glendale, CA 91201

PRESIDENTE
BRITE SMILE
490 N. Wiget Lane
Walnut Creek, CA 94598

Dear El Presidente Of Teeth Brite Smile:

Thank you for writing me with help I can have with whiter,
healthier smile. Yes, of course, I want white teeth. what's left
of them. My teeth currently are in color of Indian Corn - brown
and yellow & pointed at top.

Let me tell you what is going on in Kabobby household.
Generalissimo Tazmak has arrived from Farznazian. Military #
0409-RNBL. He is to try and make sense of what is going on in
backyard of Hamooli Kabobby and all the strife. He came on
Holland Alaskan cruise using his Platinum Card. He came with full
uniform of medals. and looked dignified as he inspected every
family member. Each lined up outside their respective boxes.
First he eyed Grandfather Bahir in front of his refrigerator
carton. he looked in there and saw what we all see: A spindle of
beef slowly cooking and his underwear on a fishing line drying.
He did not say anything but wrote in his little notebook. Then he
looked into Scott's stereo carton. Scott's strawberry stained
face has now grown to his whole head. His man breasts stood out.
Under bubble wrap was Coco Laboy. he had on tight cargo shorts &
sprinkles from Baskin Robbins ice cream glued onto his eyelids.
Tazmak arrived with Kajian L. Petgroomer, his trusted aide.
HUMMUS!!!

He then moved everybody out of their cartons and boxes & into
everyone elses cartons and boxes. He said for security reasons.
Yaggi no longer stays under umbrella bubble wrap. He is now in
Scott's stereo carton. Maheeni and Tahini are out of their egg
crate and into 34 person Bahir tent moving Coco and Shwarmi out of
that tent and into Maheeni and Tahini's crate. What is this magic
mirror you write about? Generalissimo Tazmak will find my grill.

My breath stinks. Baby Maheeni wants you to see her coloring she
made of you, Mr. Teeth Leader. There's the sun in there and
tetanus. Let's get my teeth white,

Hamooli Kabobby

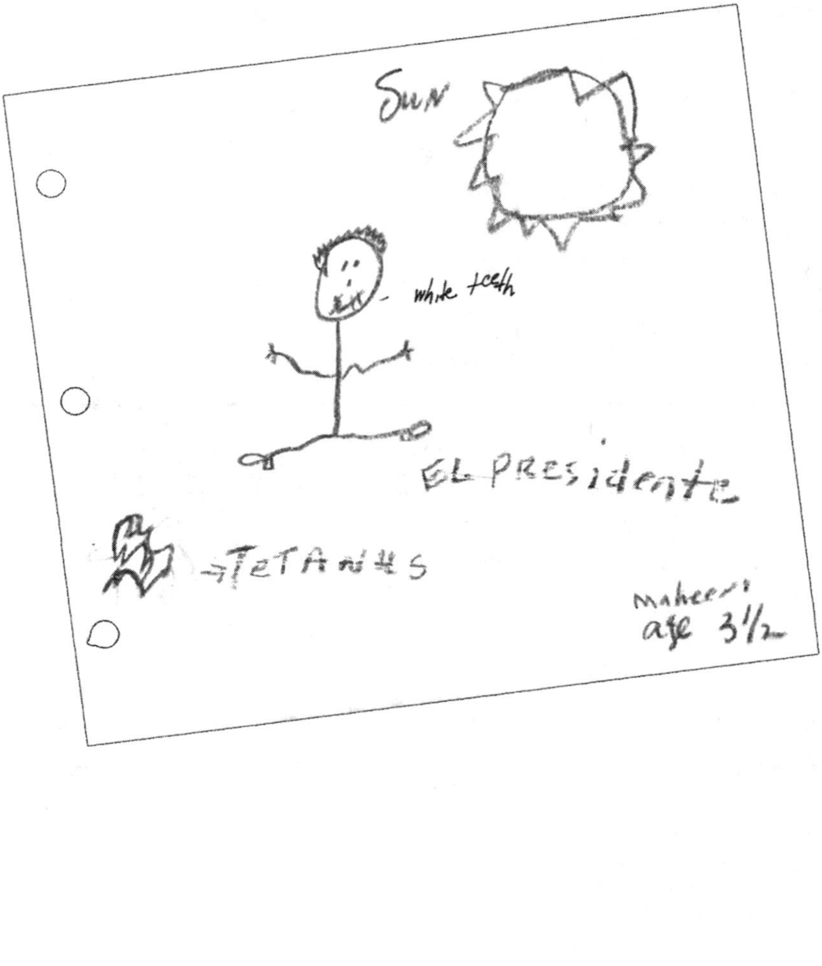

SUN

white teeth

EL PRESidente

TETANUS

maheen
age 3½

TELESCOPES.COM
30 East Superior St.
Duluth, MN 55802

Dear Telescope Peoples,

My name is not KABLOB!!! It is KABOBBY!!! Bahir Kabobby. Not bahir kablob!!!! (You said: Hello bahir kablob in your letter to me.)

Please! And also, use capital beginning letters. Thank you.

While in itself, this is not annoying, the fact i am living now under bubble wrap from umbrella makes it worse.

Plus neighbor to my right (Coco LaBoy) has set up telescope and (i believe) is looking at me. He has seen me in my underwear. The whole thought of being peeped on is disgusting.

I walk around in my underwear because it is my privilege and MY UNDERWEAR!!!! That is why I now want telescope of my own. from you. To peep on him. When can I get? Huh?

Barzannia Respect,

Bahir Kabobby (Not kablob)

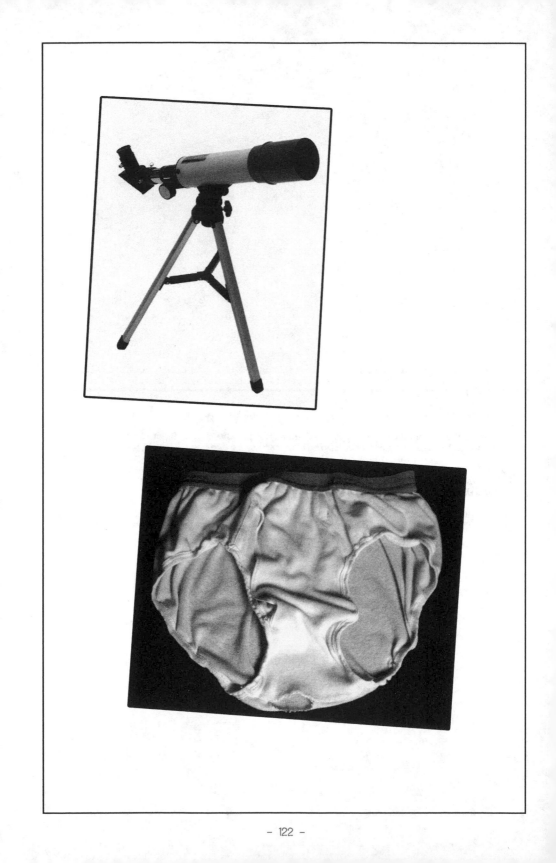

Dear Bahir,

Thank you for your email inquiry.

Thank you for visiting our website. The main thing in a telescope that will allow you to see an object beyond our solar system like galaxies etc is the aperture (or diameter) of the scope itself.

In essence, the bigger the diameter of the scope the more light you will gather. When we are looking into space all we can see is the light coming from these objects so the more area there is to collect the light, the bigger, brighter and farther we are able to see. The bigger the diameter of the scope, the better the view will be for you.

Having said this here are some links for you to look at of large scopes in different price ranges. Please feel free to email or call with any questions while you are trying to make your decision.

http://www.telescopes.com/products/zhumell-eclipse-114-with-motor-drive-21576.html

http://www.telescopes.com/products/zhumell-10-inch-dobsonian-reflector-telescope-38399.html

http://www.telescopes.com/products/meade-etx-105at-astro-telescope-uhtc-coatings-18209.html

Each of the above items is in stock and ready to ship today. So you can have the item within about a week with standard shipping.

Best regards,

VeryBestBaking.com
BAKE THE VERY BEST®

RECIPES | ADVICE | PROMOTIONS | COMMUNITY | NESTLÉ PRODUCTS

Nestlé Carnation

Learn why **CARNATION®**
Evaporated Milk is **The Cooking Milk**™

FREE CARNATION® Recipe Booklet

Receive a **FREE CARNATION recipe booklet** by
entering the Cooking Milk Sweepstakes! Everyone
who enters gets a 40-page, full color booklet full of
tempting photos and delicious new recipes for Soups,
Desserts, Entrees and more. **Click here for a sneak
peak.**
You'll also be entered for a chance to win your own
copy of **Cook Smart** in The Cooking Milk™
Sweepstakes from CARNATION!

Pear Clafouti with Cardamom Custard Sauce

Intermediate

Intermediate

Challenging

Key Lime Mousse with   "At Home" Pad Thai with   Dulce de Leche Crème

VeryBestBaking.com
P.O. Box 2178
Wilkes-Barre, PA 18703

Privacy Policy

©2006 NESTLÉ

GEELA KABOBBY
1413 1/2 Kenneth Rd.
#193
Glendale, CA 91201

VERY BEST BAKING.COM
CARNATION EVAPORATED MILK
NESTLE
PO Box 2178
Wilkes Barre, PA 18703

Dear Carnation Milks:,

Carnation Trusted Milk. Yes it is the cooking milk. I like your
picture of the Pear Clafouti with the Cardamom custard sauce. I
CURSE ALL PEAR CLAFOUTI WITH CARDAMOM CUSTARD SAUCE IF TRUTH BE
KNOWN!!!

An old Barzannian proverb say: Fear the person who doesn't fear
camel squeek. Generalissimo Tazmak is a monster, Carnation. He
has built prison out of metal and iron and grate. he has build
this prison and currently has Coco Laboy inside it. (He removed
him from his crate and put him there at 3 a:m in morning) This
prison is despicable example of human suffering. he has LaBoy in
skimpy Underoos and clothespins on his nipples for punishment. He
says it is for security reasons.

he is tyrant and wields fierceness back here. everyone is afraid
of Tazmak. Kajiian Petgroomer watches when Tazmak sleeps. He has
a closed eye. It must be infected, Carnation, with pear clafouti.
That is what doctor graduate from Le Cordron Brown say.

I like your picture of Dulce de Leche Creme. I CURSE ALL DULCE DE
LECHE CREME!!!! HASELAAAM! SEELIBAAM!!

When can i get my Carnation Recipe book? I like all powdered
foods. Tell me more of evaporated milk. I once had evaporated
salami sandwich. (it was gone. where did it go?)

Sincerely,

Geela Kabobby
Carnation Evaporated Fan

Consumer Services Center
P.O. Box 2178
Wilkes-Barre, PA 18703
VeryBestBaking.com

February 21, 2007

Geela Kabobby
1413 1/2 W Kenneth Rd # 193
Glendale, CA 91201-1478

Dear Nestlé Consumer,

Thank you for taking the time to contact us about Carnation® Evaporated Milk. We welcome questions and comments from loyal consumers such as yourself and appreciate this opportunity to assist you.

The Carnation Evaporated Milk, fondly referred to as The Cooking Milk, is often used in place of milk in cooking due to its rich flavor, creamy consistency and nutritional benefits.

Carnation Evaporated Milk is made from fresh milk which is gently heated to remove about half its water content. This special concentration of milk offers significant cooking and baking performance benefits to help recipes taste and perform better

We appreciate your interest in our products. Should you have additional questions or comments, please do not hesitate to contact us at 1-800-854-8935, Monday - Friday, 8:00 a.m. to 8:00 p.m., Eastern Time.

Sincerely,

Consumer Response Representative

P.S. We invite you to visit us at VeryBestBaking.com where you will find over 500 delicious recipes. At VeryBestBaking.com, you can create your own private recipe box, post reviews of recipes, enjoy holiday articles, discover kids' activities, and share your favorite baking memories. Nestlé and VeryBestBaking.com want to help you bake the very best!

All trademarks are owned by Société des Produits Nestlé S.A., Vevey, Switzerland.

Holland America Line
A Signature of Excellence

Customer #: 359059748
Hamooli Kabobby
1413 1/2 W Kenneth Rd # 193
Glendale, CA 91201-1478

Dear Hamooli Kabobby,

→ Huh?

Recently you should have received our full-color Panama Canal mailing featuring a large regional map, Panama Canal history and descriptions of our diverse fall 2006 and winter 2007 itineraries. If you've ever considered a Panama Canal cruise, now is a great time to book—you'll be able to choose from a wide selection of Panama Canal cruises that also journey to Central America, the Caribbean, Mexico and even the Amazon. And for a limited time, you can take advantage of special reduced fares.

Book your Panama Canal sailing by June 30 and take advantage of reduced fares of up to $800.

Holland America Line offers so many great ways to experience the Panama Canal, and for a limited time, you can save with new lower fares that have been further reduced by $100 to $800 per person on select sailings.

The Panama Canal is a "must see" on every traveler's wish list—an epic accomplishment to rival the Great Pyramids, or man's trip to the moon. Come with us on an exciting full transit from sea to sea, with days of Caribbean beaches, Costa Rican rain forests and the sunny Mexican Riviera (including our brand-new port of call, Puerto Chiapas). If your time is limited, enjoy a fascinating 10-day foray through Gatun Locks and into jungle-clad Gatun Lake, with Caribbean ports that include our private island Half Moon Cay, roundtrip from Ft. Lauderdale. Or opt to glide slowly up the Amazon past sultry river towns after completing a Panama Canal transit.

Whichever journey you choose, you'll enjoy Holland America's spacious midsized ships and enriching onboard activities including the Explorations Speaker Series (featuring a Panama Canal historian on every cruise) and cooking classes from celebrated chefs in the Culinary Arts Center, presented by *Food & Wine* magazine.

Book early for the best selection of itineraries and staterooms.

With so many exceptional ways to see the Panama Canal this fall and winter, and limited-time **savings of up to $800 per person**, now is a great time to book your once-in-a-lifetime voyage.

Choose your favorite itinerary from those on the back of this letter, then book by June 30, 2006 and save up to $800. Call your Travel Professional or 1-877-SAIL HAL, or to learn more, visit us today at www.hollandamerica.com. We look forward to welcoming you on board for one of these rare and amazing voyages.

Sincerely,

Stein Kruse
President and Chief Executive Officer

P.S. Book by June 30 and enjoy your special savings of up to $800 per person on the Panama Canal cruises on the back of this letter. Space is limited—call your Travel Professional or 1-877-SAIL HAL today.

HAMOOLI KABOBBY
1413 1/2 Kenneth Rd.
#193
Glendale, CA 91201

Stein Kruse
HOLLAND AMERICA CRUISE LINE
P.O. Box 34985
Seattle, WA 98124

Dear Mr. Stein Kruse, Holland Cruise Line,

I am in receipt of your letter to me wanting me to go to Panama
Canal. I JUST CAME BACK FROM ALASKA!!! YOU SENT ME!!! TO THE
FREEZING COLD! Now you want me to be in scorching, sweltering
heat of Panama Canal??? I almost froze my falafals off. Hoo-ee
was it cold. How can you now send me here?

Of course I will go to Panama Canal. When? I am ready. I want
it to be as hot as can be. Will you take my Vue card? I have
$121.00 left on it. (I bought felt hats for everybody in July).

Now down to problem: Help me, Holland Cruise and Stein Kruse. I
am customer number 359059748 which is coincidentally Generalissimo
Tazmak's aide Kajiian Petgroomer's military rank number.

Generalissimo Tazmak has his eye on Coco Laboy who he has
imprisoned in makeshift jail. It is behind Bahir's old
refrigerator carton. It is made of metal with lock on it. Today
Coco has sparklie blue eye shadow on and is in hip hugger capri
clamdigger pants. They are very, very tight. (That is 2 verys).
The backside is cut out in a heart shape hole revealing red
buttocks. (What went on back there? You tell me Holland Cruise)

Shwarmi is restless over Coco. So is Yaggi. My yard is becoming
a gay swamp. Tazmak is fearless in his commanding. To continue
my newsletter: My son Scott now has: huge man tits, no hair on
his head, hair all over his back from reading directions wrong on
"where to apply" from hair restoration peoples, and he smokes like
Turkish chimney. Scott is big mess. SHALEELAMM!

Re: Panama Canal: I am booking by June 30 to take advantage as
you ask me to. Do we still need a boat? Let's get me going!

Traveling Man,

Hamooli Kabobby

- 129 -

Holland America Line
P.O. Box 34985
Seattle, WA 98124

Guest ID# 359059748
Hamooli Kabobby
1413 1/2 W Kenneth Rd # 193
Glendale CA 91201-1478

A Signature of Ex

The cruise materials you requested have arrived.

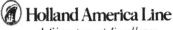
Holland America Line
A Signature of Excellence

Guest ID# 359059748
Hamooli Kabobby
1413 1/2 W Kenneth Rd # 193
Glendale CA 91201-1478

Take your expectations up a notch and experience Holland America.

Dear Hamooli Kabobby,

There are cruises, and then there are Holland America cruises. Something altogether different—a step above, a step apart, composed of things both large and small. Fresh-cut flowers, the surprise delivery of your favorite beverage by a smiling waiter, a stateroom so spacious it makes you feel right at home (only with perpetually fresh towels.)

It's a quality you'll find everywhere you go on a Holland America ship. Starting from the personalized attention you receive from our highly trained crew members (more per guest than any other cruise line in our class) and continuing to the deluxe amenities…the full-service spa… the museum-quality artwork…the diverse dining options…and award-winning entertainment that make your days and nights on board something beyond special. It's no wonder Holland America is consistently rated among the world's best cruise lines by *Condé Nast Traveler* and *Travel + Leisure*.

Whether your vacation is for pure relaxation or to explore a fascinating part of the world, you can be assured that we have what the most discerning traveler wants. After all, we've spent more than 130 years identifying what goes into the perfect cruise vacation. Which means, you can experience the Holland America difference the minute you begin your booking.

Discover how you can save on current brochure rates.

Who says that an incredible cruise can't also be an incredible value? Call your travel professional or 1-877-SAIL HAL (1-877-724-5425) for today's best cruise fares and you'll discover ways to save on our current brochure prices. You'll still get all the same extras that make a Holland America cruise special: more space, more award-winning service, more intriguing ways to explore your world. Plus, you'll see savings that allow you to upgrade to a luxury Verandah Suite, extend your voyage or add on a pre- or post-cruise package.

It's time to expect more from a cruise. It's time for Holland America.

Sincerely,

Stein Kruse
President and Chief Executive Officer

P.S. Come discover the Holland America difference. Call your travel professional or 1-877-SAIL HAL (1-877-724-5425) today to receive the best fares, itineraries and staterooms.

Click Here To Get Started!

Dear HAMOOLI,

Hello! I am the Vice President of Nutrition Services for eDiets.com. Congratulations on taking the first step toward living a healthier lifestyle by completing a Personal Diet Profile! I know that you could benefit greatly by becoming an eDiets.com member.

Now for a limited time, you can join eDiets.com for just $2.99 - but you must act before midnight, May 31, 2004!

You get:

> **Your choice of 17 diet plans** which includes the proven-successful eDiets Weight Loss Plan plus a range of Healthy Living diets that address specific concerns, such as high cholesterol or Type 2 diabetes. We can even customize the Zone Perfect Diet, Atkins Nutritional Approach^{TM}, and Slim·Fast® programs just for you!

> **A customized weekly meal plan** to fit your lifestyle and food preferences – whether you prefer to cook all your meals or need to eat "on the run"

> **Weekly grocery lists** to make shopping a breeze

> **Personal support and encouragement** from my colleagues at Support Central, plus a robust network of mentors and fellow dieters eager to help you reach your goals

> **Advice from licensed behavioral psychologists** that can help you identify and overcome any emotional obstacles to living a healthier lifestyle

> **Plus a host of support tools** to give you the extra motivation, skills and knowledge you need to reach your goal!

For most people, maintaining a healthy weight is a never-ending battle. eDiets.com gives you the tools and support you need to WIN that battle – for life. (Just check out these testimonials for living proof!)

So, what are you waiting for? Now's the time to get on your way to a healthier, happier life!

Best wishes for your success,

Vice President of Nutrition Services

HAMOOLI KABOBBY
1413 1/2 Kenneth Rd.
#193
Glendale, CA 91201

MRS. VICE PRESIDENT OF:
E DIETS.COM
3801 W Hillsboro Blvd
Deerfield Beach, FL 33442

Dear Mrs. Vice President,

Yes I am ready to lose weight. I am currently living on 37 packs
of gum a day. I have taste of spearmint permanently in my mouth.
Yesterday I belched up pimento. Where that came from I do not
know. (maybe from meal in '97)

Generalissimo Tazmak has ripped apart my shanty backyard. he is
madman looking for grill. I say it is gone forever. He has
screamed at Grandfather Bahir and blamed him for theft of the
grill. An offense in the Feezi legal system. (I studied law at
Feezi University and while at FU I wrote two briefs. One to Mr. G
at Indymac Bank) Tazmak has been flogging Coco LaBoy with flogger
he made out of palm fronds and gym sock. Coco squirms and
thrashes about in his jail as Tazmak lashes him. Then he tickles
him for 20 minutes. What kind of punishment is this?

Bahir has Rotweiller eyes at inference he stole my grill. Where
is it, MS Vice President of Ediets.com? (what does dot mean? i'm
on a need to know basis) Grandfather Bahir spends all day in his
lettuce crate watching Judge Joe Brown and festering over Judge's
decisions. Bahir's extension cord sparks. I hate Judge Joe
Brown. He ruled against me once on wig I bought in Bollywood.
The netting sweated up. Baby Maheeni now weighs 200 pounds. Can
she be helped? She is 41 months old and eats nothing but
Fudgesickles.

Is there more then 17 diet plans? I was looking for 20. I am
worried about: A. my grill. B. Grandfather Bahir and his Joe
Brown decision festering. C. Coco LaBoy and his tubercular cough.
Let's work together to get everyone down to size 58 waist. Scott
is wheezing toward finish line. Help me.

Sincerely,

Hamooli Kabobby
Hamooli Kabobby

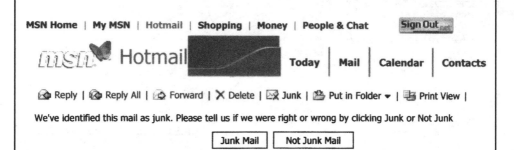

Today | **Mail** | **Calendar** | **Contacts**

📩 Reply | 📩 Reply All | 📩 Forward | ✖ Delete | 📨 Junk | 📇 Put in Folder ▾ | 🖨 Print View |

We've identified this mail as junk. Please tell us if we were right or wrong by clicking Junk or Not Junk

Junk Mail		Not Junk Mail

Hello coco kablob!

We have successfully added your email address to the e-metal-detectors.com newsletter.
Just for signing up, enter this coupon code **65323** when shopping at our site and recive $5.00
off any order over $50.00! In our newsletters you will be the first to be informed about coupons and
closeout deals offered by e-metal-detectors.com. Your privacy is of utmost importance to us. e-metal-
detectors.com does not sell its email lists. We also keep your information safe by continually updating and
contracting third party companies to simulate hacking on our servers. This commitment to security keeps
your personal information safe.

Please feel free to contact us at any time,
e-metal-detectors.com
30 East Superior St.
Duluth MN 55802
info@e-metal-detectors.com

COCO LaBOY c/o
KABOBBY
1413 1/2 Kenneth Rd.
#193
Glendale, CA 91201

METAL DETECTORS
30 East Superior St.
Duluth, MN 55802

Dear Metal Detectors:

My name's not KABLOB!!! It is Coco LaBoy. Not Coco Kablob. You
wrote me as coco kablob. And puleeze use capital letters when
using someone's name. It's just proper grammar, you know.

When can I get a metal detector? I am in a prison that I do not
want to be in. This Generalissimo Tazmak is a nasty man. he has
big hands. He has singled me out to be in his stupid homemade
prison. I did not take that moronic grill. Who cares???

Generalissimo Tazmak is determined to bring order to this infected
mess of a backyard but all he is doing is moving people around.
He announced today his hard labor plan: if the grill does not turn
up then everyone will dig ditches until it does while he and that
dumb Kajiian Petgroomer dude watch us.

Personally, metal detector people, I think he just likes to see a
bunch of men without shirts on working in the hot sun and
sweating. Hamooli is a Co*ksu*ker. He can go Fu*k himself and
that stupid pig grill he says he paid $2,400 for. He should have
used the money for medical needs for his fat son Scott who is a
mess. He has shreds of hair on weird places on his body and has
terrible foot odor. I think he smokes like 6 packs a day now.
Pheewww! His lung must be hanging on like a trapeze artist.

I believe this prison Generalissimo Tazmak built out of iron and
grate looks suspiciously like Hamooli's grill. I am being held
against my will by a mad dictator. (With big hands)

Help me,

Coco LaBoy

COCO LaBOY HAS RUN OFF WITH GENERALISSIMO TAZMAK!

ASIAN DATING

Dear Baby Kabobby,

Thank you for registering. You are now a member of our site!

We encourage you to create a profile and upload as many photos as you can - the more the better, it increases your chances of being contact by someone else!

You can sign in to your account by clicking here and using the following login information:
Username: freekie
Password: fudgieman

Thank you again, and we hope you enjoy your visit.

HAMOOLI KABOBBY
1413 1/2 Kenneth Rd.
#193
Glendale, CA 91201

ASIAN DATING
AsianDating@5labs.com

Dear Asian Dating Peoples

DATING?! Baby Kabobby is 41 months old. (She weighs 211 pounds) She only eats Philly Cheese Steaks from Pats Steaks. How dare you insult Baby Maheeni? I curse you with 1000 camel hairs!

There must me some mistake. USERNAME: FREEKIE?! PASSWORD: FUDGIEMAN?! What is going on here???? Let's work together to esponge Baby Maheeni from your dating site. It is just not right.

Respectfully,

Hamooli Kabobby
Father

SHWARMI KABOBBY
1413 1/2 Kenneth Rd.
#193
Glendale, CA 91201

Dating Peoples
MATCH.COM
PO Box 25472
Dallas, TX 75225

Dear Match Dot Com Peoples.

I must confess, Me, Shwarmi Kabobby, I am BIGFATGAL. I am also
receiving mail at Asian Dating that I enroll under using BABY
MAHEENI'S name. I am sick and need help. But I also want to meet
singles!!!

Coco has run of with Generalissimo Tazmak. Where are they? You
tell me, Match Dot Com. Tazmak took the boyman from my umbrella
and they left. At 3 a:m. Coco was wearing flexible fit t-shirt &
butt huggers with revolutionary moisture wicking cotton? From
Macy's??? (it is me Ted. I am Shwarmi. I'm inside him now.)

So now it is time for me to move on and meet new peoples. Can you
help me, Match peoples? I am 52 years old and have goat with
infected teats. but goat has salve on 5 of them as we speak. I
also like shrimp deveining, tobacco stench, and swimsuit netting.

Is anyone out there for me? My ears are all cleaned out. Tazmak
will only mess up Coco's head not like me who has read Chinese
poems for him in past. Grandfather Bahir is fooling around with
ravioli recipes. Why? Keep eye on him.

Let's get me started in dating world!!!

No Respect For Tazmak,

Shwarmi Kabobby
Shwarmi Kabobby

SHWARMI KABOBBY
1413 1/2 Kenneth Rd.
#193
Glendale, CA 91201

Dear Match Dot Com Peoples.

Thank you for speedy answer and selection of fine peoples for me
to meets. It's me - BIG FAT GAL. (Shwarmi Kabobby) And yes i am
interested in your mens matches. How can we meet? Do i send a
wink? How about a stare? I must tell you -- Hamooli's sister,
Feroozi has flushed yet another of his relatives out of Turkish
sewer system and he's on way to America. I believe he plans to
live in Sandwich, Louisiana. Feroozi is fine woman with mole and
hair in it.

Coco LaBoy has returned to backyard with Generalissimo Tazmak and
they are giving me cold ~~collarbone~~ shoulder. They know that I
know what they know. and that is that COCO IS MY FRIEND AND
SHOULDN'T HAVE LEFT WITH HIM!!! It's as simple as that, Match Dot
Coms. They have taken up residence in Scott's former stereo
crate. Scott has a few strands of hair on his head. I want to
meet everyones in your ad. How?

Grandfather Bahir is fooling around with some ravioli recipes.
Why? Keep an eye on him.

Shwarmi Kabobby
BIGFATGAL

Thank you for recently visiting www.trojancondoms.com and requesting your free sample. You can be confident knowing that TROJAN® Brand Condoms have been Triple Tested for quality and protection. Trojan is America's #1 condom and has been trusted for over 80 years.

With proper use, Trojan will provide the pleasure you want and the protection you trust. With 20 different condom choices in a variety of shapes, sizes and materials, you're sure to find the one that is right for you and your partner. Besides abstinence, condoms are the only means to help reduce the transmission of Sexually Transmitted Diseases (STDs), while also being highly effective at preventing pregnancy.

If you did not request this sample, please notify us in writing at the below address and we will ensure a sample cannot be requested in your name in the future:

Trojan Consumer Relations
469 N. Harrison Street
Princeton, NJ 08543

For more facts and information on our products and how to use them, please visit
www.trojancondoms.com.
You can also get additional information about safer sexual health at
www.trojaninfocenter.com. Thank you again for requesting your free sample!

Best regards,

TROJAN® Brand Condoms

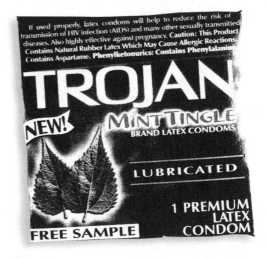

COCO LaBOY c/o
HAMOOLI KABOBBY
1413 1/2 Kenneth Rd.
#193
Glendale, CA 91201

TROJAN CONDOMS
P.O. Box 200
Young America, MN 55553-0200

Dear Trojan Condoms,

I am looking at your Trojan rubber now. I am delighted. How can
I receive more condoms? Only mint, please. I tried your caramel
condoms and the caramel and rubber stuck to the roof of my mouth.

Generalissimo Tazmak removed me from his jail at 3:30 a:m this
morning. he took me with his big hands and unlocked my prison.
He took me off. He hurried me away. Shwarmi & Yaggi watched with
what i know is envy in their eyes. I was helpless to do anything
with such a forceful military leader. His medals pricked me.

Yes I am active, Trojan. Yaggi knows that Shwarmi and I are in
his carton a lot. But no more. where will i be taken? This is a
mess back here in this swampy backyard. There is disease
everywhere. Weird blotches are breaking out on people. I wish
things were different. There is no sewage and it smells. People
wash up with a hose then drink from it. It is disgusting.

Let's get me some more condoms. These are the flavors i request:
Cherry, lemon, new car. I only use Trojan condoms. Is there any
other kind? I can't open the package.

For a safe world,

Coco LaBoy

March 7, 2007

Mr. Coco Laboy
Hamooli Kabobby
1413 1/2 W Kenneth Rd
Glendale, CA 91201-1478

Dear Mr. Laboy:

Thank you for contacting us recently to let us know you enjoy using Trojan®
Condoms.

At Church & Dwight Co., Inc., we strive to manufacture products of high
quality and performance that meet genuine consumer needs. It is gratifying
to learn from you that our efforts are recognized and appreciated.

You are able to request one condom sample per year from our web site at
www.trojancondoms.com. We are unable to provide you with any other samples.

Again, thank you for taking the time and having the interest to contact us.

Cordially,

Consumer Relations Representative

 ARRID Brillo CLEAN SHOWER CLOSE-UP FIRST RESPONSE Lambert Kay Mentadent Nair SCRUB FREE

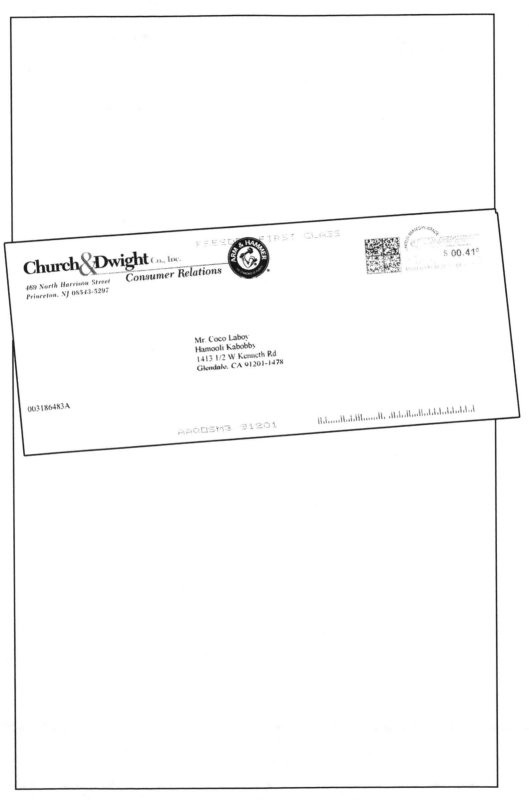

Church&Dwight Co., Inc.
Consumer Relations
469 North Harrison Street
Princeton, NJ 08543-5297

PRESORTED FIRST CLASS

ARM & HAMMER
THE STANDARD OF PURITY

UNITED STATES POSTAGE
$ 00.41°

Mr. Coco Laboy
Hamooli Kabobby
1413 1/2 W Kenneth Rd
Glendale, CA 91201-1478

003186483A

AACDSMB 91201

SECOND NOTICE

THANK YOU FOR YOUR ORDER INSTRUCTIONS. PLEASE
USE THIS INVOICE FOR ANY LABEL CORRECTIONS.

Dear Geela Kabobby,

Again, our thanks to you for subscribing to *The Economist*. We trust your
weekly issues are now arriving regularly.

In future issues, we urge you to pay particular attention to our business and
political analyses. There are certain to be important indicators valuable to your
reading.

Will you please take a moment now, if you haven't already, to check that our
last invoice hasn't been overlooked. If your payment is in the mail, many
thanks for your efficiency. If perchance it hasn't been sent, won't you please
enclose your payment in the pre-addressed envelope we've provided and mail it
straightaway. We need to receive your payment in the next few days in order
to continue sending your issues. Thank you.

Sincerely,

Hilde Sprung
Hilde Sprung
Circulation Subscriptions Director

The Economist Newspaper North America, Inc.
Subscription Department, PO Box 50402, Boulder, CO 80322-0402   800-456-6086

The Economist Subscription Center at www.economist.com/subcenter

GEELA KABOBBY
1413 1/2 Kenneth Rd.
#193
Glendale, CA 91201

THE ECONOMIST MAGAZINE
P.O. Box 50402
Boulder, Colorodo
80322-0402

Dear Economist:

Re: Your 2nd notice to me. I am sad. I have no money. It blew
away. Yet I like reading your magazine. I thumb through it. I
have no thumb. It blew away.

FYI i have been paying particular attentions to your business &
political analysis. I CURSE ALL BUSINESS & POLITICAL ANALYSIS!!
HASSELEMM! My son Scott smoke 12 packs of Viceroys a day. He has
1/2 lung which is hanging on like squirrel on branch. His hair on
back is red and and his face blushes. He looks like cheap carpet.
I CURSE ALL CHEAP CARPETS EVERYWHERE!!!

I enjoy your magazine. When will my next issue arrive? Yes, they
are arriving regularly. I checked and your last invoice hasn't
been overlooked. Your magazine is my only joy. I can't open
wrapper.

With Respect For The Economist,

Geela Kabobby
Geela Kabobby
Sad

international male

YOUR ACCOUNT
SIGN IN

SEARCH
[   ] GO

SHOPPI
0 item
check

E-mail
Newsletter | Place a
Catalog Order | Shop Our
Virtual Catalog | FREE Delivery
Advantage Club℠

About Us   FAQ's   Fit Chart   FREE Catalog   Affiliate Program   Email A Friend   order

Suits
Underwear
Woven Shirts
Knit Shirts
Sweaters
Sets
Outerwear
Leather
Jackets
Jeans
Pants
Shorts
Swimwear
Activewear
Lounge
Shoes
Accessories
Skincare
Join Our Clubs
On Sale Now!

Underwear: **Problem Solvers**

email a friend

◀ previous   next ▶

Go Softwear® Padded Butt Boxer Brief
With new lower prices, it's easier than ever
to get the fuller, rounder silhouette you want.
Backside padding enhances your rear view.
2" inseam, logo waistband. Cotton/Lycra®
spandex. Machine wash. USA.

ON SALE!

Due to the nature of this incredible promotion, we
apologize that no other promotions or discounts will
be accepted on these items.

Color and sizes sell out fast, check the drop down
menus on the left for availability. Some items may no
longer be available when order is processed.

Go Softwear® Padded Butt Boxer Brief
Check availability
AE21
ON SALE! $30.00 (Regular Price: $39.99)

SIZE   [SELECT ▾]
COLOR   [SELECT ▾]

add to

COCO LaBOY c/o
HAMOOLI KABOBBY
1413 1/2 Kenneth Rd.
#193
Glendale, CA 91201

INTERNATIONAL MALE
1500 Harbor Blvd
Weehawken, NJ 07086

Dear International Male,

Who is in that picture? Is his name Ryan? I'm sure I saw him at
Leopard. I'd like to use a lemon condom on...NOT GOING THERE!!!

Generalissimo Tazmak drove me around in his car for 13 straight
hours. I said "Where are we going?" Finally we stopped at a
Burger King. I ate a burger. The backyard is more depressing
then ever. Yaggi's been drinking Morgan's Rum and squints his eye
like the pirate on the bottle. But it stays closed. My sister in
Wisconsin has herpes.

How can I get that picture of Ryan enlarged? (The padded butt
boxer brief one) Maybe a 6 foot by 9 foot enlargement. Without
distorting the print?

Generalissimo has been very strong with me. He got me a little
kings crown at Burger King. It still has lettuce on it. I wore
it last night and it glowed in the dark. He said i was king.
Sometimes I miss Wisconsin. But where will i live there?

I think that dumb Shwarmi's joined a dating service under the name
PLASTIC SPORK IN MY BRA. Isn't that the combination fork-spoon at
KFC? Who would contact him with that name??? The only other
worse name for a dating handle is ELONGATED NIPPLES. Where's my
underwear? I paid for it with walnuts.

Respect for Ryan and his padded butt,

Coco LaBoy
Happy

international male®

February 21, 2007

Coco LaBoy
Hamooli Kaobby
1413 ½ Kenneth Rd. #193
Glendale. CA 91201

Dear Customer.

We are writing in reference to your recent inquiry to International Male®. Thank you for contacting us with your concern.

We are not showing record of the order you inquired about. In order for us to further research and/or replace your order. please provide us with proof of purchase, along with a copy of what you ordered.

If you paid by check and this check has been cashed, please forward a clear copy of the **front and back** endorsements. If the billing of this order has been billed to your credit card already, please forward a copy of the statement showing this transaction.

We apologize for any inconvenience. We will work quickly and accurately to resolve this issue for you. Should you have any concerns, please do not hesitate to contact us. We look forward to hearing from you soon.

Sincerely.

INTERNATIONAL MALE®
340 POPLAR STREET
HANOVER PA 17333-0001

S 00.41°

Coco LaBoy
1413 ½ Kenneth Rd.
Glendale. CA 91201

9120151421 C008

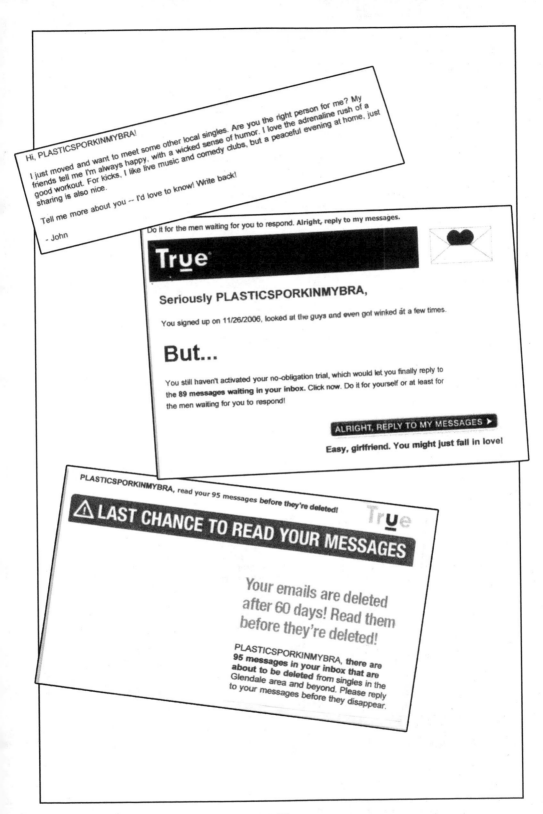

Hi, PLASTICSPORKINMYBRA!

I just moved and want to meet some other local singles. Are you the right person for me? My friends tell me I'm always happy, with a wicked sense of humor. I love the adrenaline rush of a good workout. For kicks, I like live music and comedy clubs, but a peaceful evening at home, just sharing is also nice.

Tell me more about you -- I'd love to know! Write back!

- John

Do it for the men waiting for you to respond. Alright, reply to my messages.

True°

Seriously PLASTICSPORKINMYBRA,

You signed up on 11/26/2006, looked at the guys and even got winked at a few times.

But...

You still haven't activated your no-obligation trial, which would let you finally reply to the **89 messages waiting in your inbox.** Click now. Do it for yourself or at least for the men waiting for you to respond!

ALRIGHT, REPLY TO MY MESSAGES ▶

Easy, girlfriend. You might just fall in love!

PLASTICSPORKINMYBRA, read your 95 messages before they're deleted!

True°

⚠ LAST CHANCE TO READ YOUR MESSAGES

Your emails are deleted after 60 days! Read them before they're deleted!

PLASTICSPORKINMYBRA, there are **95 messages in your inbox that are about to be deleted** from singles in the Glendale area and beyond. Please reply to your messages before they disappear.

- 151 -

Welcome, ELONGATEDNIPPLES!

Log in to Activate Your Account

Dear ELONGATEDNIPPLES,

Thank you for joining German FriendFinder, **located at**
http://germanfriendfinder.com.

Log in **now with your handle and password to activate your account and start
meeting new and intriguing members right away:**

Handle: ELONGATEDNIPPLES

You can also log in automatically using this link:

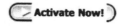

To change this password to one that's easier for you to remember, log in, **click
on the "My Account" link in the nav bar and then on the "Password" link in the
Account box.**

Please note that your profile will not be visible to other members until you log in
for the first time to activate your account.

If you have any questions, please feel free to contact us.

Thank you,

**The German FriendFinder Team
"Please Tell a Friend about** German FriendFinder!"

This email was sent to you in association with the member, ELONGATEDNIPPLES, on
German FriendFinder, using the following information:

Location: Glendale, California,
Intro: GERMAN NITWIT WITH PHGLEM

If you think you've received this email in error, you may remove your email address from our
database.

German FriendFinder, 445 Sherman Avenue, Suite C, Palo Alto, CA 94306

GermanFriendFinder.com

Your Profile on German FriendFinder has been Denied

Dear ELONGATEDNIPPLES,

We are sorry to inform you that the profile you created on German FriendFinder has been denied due to the following reason:

- Your handle was inappropriate.

Please contact Customer Service at http://germanfriendfinder.com/p/help.cgi?contact=1&lfrom=pd **for assistance.**

Sincerely,

The German FriendFinder Team
http://germanfriendfinder.com

German FriendFinder
445 Sherman Avenue, Suite C
Palo Alto, CA 94306

If you forgot your password, please go to http://germanfriendfinder.com/go/page/forgot_login.html

For any other questions, or to contact us, please go to http://germanfriendfinder.com/p/help.cgi?contact=1&lfrom=pd

This email was sent to you in association with the member, ELONGATEDNIPPLES, on German FriendFinder, **as the result of a registration on 12/25/06:16:51:1 from IP address: 66.215.13.13** using the following information:

Location: Glendale, California, 91201
Intro: GERMAN NITWIT WITH PHGLEM

If you think you've received this email in error, you may remove your email address from our database.

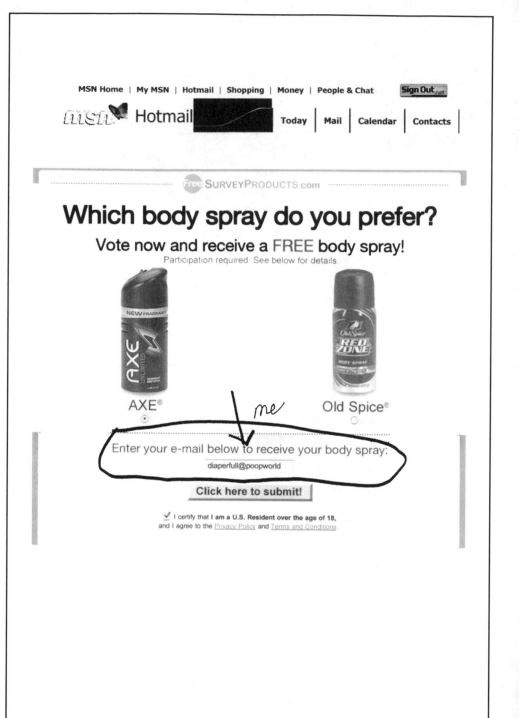

SHWARMI KABOBBY
1413 1/2 Kenneth Rd.
#193
Glendale, CA 91201

TO;   BODY SPRAY SURVEY:

You ask which body spray do i like? I say not now.   I am trying
to meet someone. It is me DIAPERFULL AT POOPWORLD.

Shwarmi

Dear Scott Kabobby,

Thank you for inquiring about Hyperhidrosis and Facial Blushing.

Dr. Malekmehr performs the clamping ETS/ ESB procedure, which is specifically tailored to your symptoms. This procedure has changed many lives, opening doors to new opportunities both professionally and socially. The details of this procedure are described at www.endsweat.com/ets.html .

This procedure is very successful in treating hyperhidrosis and facial blushing. It takes about one hour to perform and is done on an outpatient basis. The recovery is very fast. People can resume most activities in a few days. If you are coming from out of town, you should plan on being in Los Angeles for about 2-3 days.

Dr. Malekmehr personally performs all the procedure himself. He is board certified in thoracic surgery. He is also a member of the American Medical association, California Medical Association, The Society of the Thoracic Surgeons and a Fellow of the American College of Surgeons.

ETS/ESB is covered by most insurance carriers. In order to verify your insurance eligibility, please fax or email a copy of the information on the front and back of your insurance card to (866-741-5572). For those paying cash, there is a monthly payment plan available.

If you have any specific questions or would like to speak to Dr. Malekmehr for a phone consultation, please call or e-mail us.

Thank you,

California Institute for Hyperhidrosis and Facial Blushing

SCOTT KABOBBY
1413 1/2 Kenneth Rd.
#193
Glendale, CA 91201

Information.
CALIFORNIA INSTITUTE FOR FACIAL BLUSHING

Hello Doctor of Face Flush Place:

I have facial blushing. After looking up my symptoms on the Internet I got 24 porno sites and you. Will your treatment interfere with my ape like posture? My face is permanently strawberry from a Penn Foster Freeze School milkshake machine accident. It left 92 percent of my face a pinkish color with dark seed like spots in it. And a green stem on my head. When I blush I look like I have been living on the Sun.

I am getting suspicious of Generalissimo Tazmak. Something about him does not seem right. He blames Grandfather Bahir for the grill gone but I have my suspicions it is him that took it. I sweat like a pig at a luau. what can be done, Dr. Midgee? Grandfather Bahir found something weird behind Geela's plastic wrap home. It was medium size and brown with red in it. What is it?

In addition, Generalissimo's wife Yimmee is coming to America for a stomach stapling, stomach collating, and stomach 3 hole punch. I told her not to travel with Diet Wink as it is a liquid and not allowed on airplanes. I recently had to leave my Sugar Free Mountain Dew off a Jet Brown Fun flight to Peet, Arizona.

Will Yimmee think: A. My suspicions her husband is a thief. B. He has been with cheap Coco, Wisconsin street trash?

Let's get my face back to some human color.

Thank you,

Scott Kabobby

Subject : California Institute for Hyperhidrosis and Facial Blushing

Dear Scott Kabobby,

**Thank you for your recent interest about Hyperhidrosis and
Facial blushing!** We have been unsuccessful in our attempts
to contact you regarding scheduling a complimentary
consultation with Dr Malekmehr.

If you have any specific questions or would like to speak
to Dr. Malekmehr for a phone consultation, please call or
e-mail us. Dr. Malekmehr performs the clamping ETS/ ESB
procedure, which is specifically tailored to your
symptoms.

This procedure is very successful in treating
hyperhidrosis and facial blushing. It takes about one hour
to perform and is done on an outpatient basis. The
recovery is very fast. People can resume most activities
in a few days. Dr. Malekmehr personally performs all the
procedure himself. He is board certified in thoracic
surgery. He is also a member of the American Medical
association, California Medical Association, The Society
of the Thoracic Surgeons and a Fellow of the American
College of Surgeons.

Thank you,

California Institute for Hyperhidrosis
and Facial Blushing

Reader's Digest
PO BOX 7823
RED OAK, IA 51591-0823

BILL *Magazine Subscription*

BILLING DATE: November 14, 2006

RDA0698448826062760612224400998

```
12   BA2
|||....||.||.|||....|||..||
GEELA KABOBBY
1413 12 W KENNETH RD 193
GLENDALE      CA 91201
```

D

YOUR ACCOUNT NUMBER
0698448826

B06411P02

Enter
amount of
payment
enclosed ▶

AMOUNT DUE
$9.98

MAKE CHECK PAYABLE TO READER'S DIGEST AND RETURN BEFORE ▶ December 02, 2006

▼ DETACH HERE AND RETURN THIS PORTION WITH YOUR PAYMENT ▼   RDA 11/17/06 RDABL002 END905 22724

0698448826

November 14, 2006

REMINDER BILL

Amount Due $9.98
Product Supplied: Magazine Subscription Renewal

IF YOU HAVE SETTLED THIS
ACCOUNT SINCE
Nov 14, 2006
PLEASE IGNORE THIS BILL

K
E
E
P

T
H
I
S

S
E
C
T
I
O
N

GEELA KABOBBY
1413 12 W KENNETH RD 193
GLENDALE   CA 91201

CUSTOMER NUMBER
0698448826

TO GEELA KABOBBY:

HAVE YOU ALREADY SENT PAYMENT FOR YOUR READER'S
DIGEST MAGAZINE SUBSCRIPTION? IF SO, THIS NOTE IS
TO SAY "THANK YOU" FOR YOUR PROMPTNESS.
IF YOU HAVEN'T SENT YOUR PAYMENT YET, WON'T YOU
PLEASE DO IT TODAY? JUST MAIL YOUR CHECK ALONG
IN THE PRE-ADDRESSED REPLY ENVELOPE — AND WE'LL
MARK YOUR ACCOUNT "PAID." TO HELP US BRING YOU
THE BEST SERVICE, MAIL THE ENCLOSED STATEMENT
WITH YOUR PAYMENT. THANK YOU.

PRICE
* * * * * * $9.98

BALANCE
* * * * * * $9.98

Carolyn Davis

P.S. IF YOU'VE RECENTLY SENT YOUR MAGAZINE SUBSCRIP-
TION PAYMENT, PLEASE DISREGARD THIS BILL.

GEELA KABOBBY
1413 1/2 Kenneth Rd.
#193
Glendale, CA 91201

READERS DIGEST Magazine
PO Box 7823
Red Oak, IA 515-91-0823

Dear Readers Digest.

RE: REMINDER BILL. I DON'T NEED NO REMINDERS THAT I HAVE NO
MONEY!!! I AM AWARE OF THAT! It blew away. I used your pre
addressed reply envelope to send aways for Country Magazine. I
changed your address to Country Magazine address and addressed it
to Larry in Big Sandy, Texas. I CURSE ALL OF BIG SANDY, TEXAS!!!

Now down to MY business: My son Scott is a lox. I am just
realizing that now. He has: man teaties, no hairs on head, lot of
hairs on his disgusting back, facial blushing, and smokes 16 packs
of L&M's a day. He has the cough of fireman running out of
burning building. Sometime he stay awake another hour so he can
smoke more cigarette. (Only L&M.) Scott Kabobby is currently
carrying D average at the Ballpoint Penn Foster Freeze Academy
where he study pothole repair. 2 day ago he pulled tar machine
down on his head. it stuck his head together. He stuck himself
to metal rake and was rigid for 13 hours. This threw Grandfather
Bahir into rage and he said, "Your son is a fozzi. He tarred
himself solid like a pothole."

Scott's refrigerator carton is wet on one side from sprinklers.
It will collapse. He is herring. Hamooli is in Panama Canal and
says hi.

When will my next Reader's Digest magazine come? I like your
section: "Have You An Amusing Anecdote About Chinch Bugs?" I
CURSE ALL MAGAZINE AND THEIR AMUSING ANECDOTE SECTIONS!!
HASSELLOM!!! HASSHEAMM!!! My credit is zero from marrying into
this family.

Thank you,

Geela Kabobby
Reminder
Reminder

Reader's Digest
PO BOX 7823
RED OAK, IA 51591-0823

PO BOX 7823
RED OAK, IA 51591-0823

BILL *Magazine Subscription*

BILLING DATE: December 12, 2006

RDA069844882606276061222440099800000000000P0305

13 BA2

GEELA KABOBBY
1413 12 W KENNETH RD 193
GLENDALE   CA 91201

D

YOUR ACCOUNT NUMBER
0698448826

B0641IP03

Enter
amount of
payment
enclosed

AMOUNT DUE
$9.98

MAKE CHECK PAYABLE TO READER'S DIGEST AND RETURN BEFORE ▶ December 30, 2006

▼ DETACH HERE AND RETURN THIS PORTION WITH YOUR PAYMENT ▼

RDA 12/14/06 RDABL002 ETWY0S 23472

0698448826

December 12, 2006

REMINDER BILL

Amount Due $9.98	IF YOU HAVE SETTLED THIS ACCOUNT SINCE
Product Supplied: Magazine Subscription	Dec 12, 2006 PLEASE IGNORE THIS BILL

K
E
E
P

GEELA KABOBBY
1413 12 W KENNETH RD 193
GLENDALE   CA 91201

CUSTOMER NUMBER
0698448826

T
H
I
S

S
E
C
T
I
O
N

TO GEELA KABOBBY:

HAVE YOU BEEN AWAY? I'VE JUST FOUND YOUR NAME
AMONG OUR "PAST DUE" ACCOUNTS, SHOWING THAT YOU
HAVEN'T PAID FOR YOUR READER'S DIGEST SUBSCRIPTION.

IS ANYTHING WRONG? IF YOU MISLAID THE PREVIOUS BILL,
HERE IS ANOTHER THAT SHOWS EXACTLY WHAT YOU OWE.
JUST MAIL THIS BILL BACK TO ME--WITH YOUR CHECK OR
MONEY ORDER—SO I CAN MARK YOUR ACCOUNT "PAID IN
FULL." I WOULD APPRECIATE IT IF YOU WOULD SEND YOUR
PAYMENT AS SOON AS POSSIBLE.

PRICE
•••••• $9.98

BALANCE
•••••• $9.98

Sarah Gross

P.S. IF YOU'VE RECENTLY SENT YOUR MAGAZINE SUBSCRIPTION
PAYMENT, PLEASE DISREGARD THIS BILL.

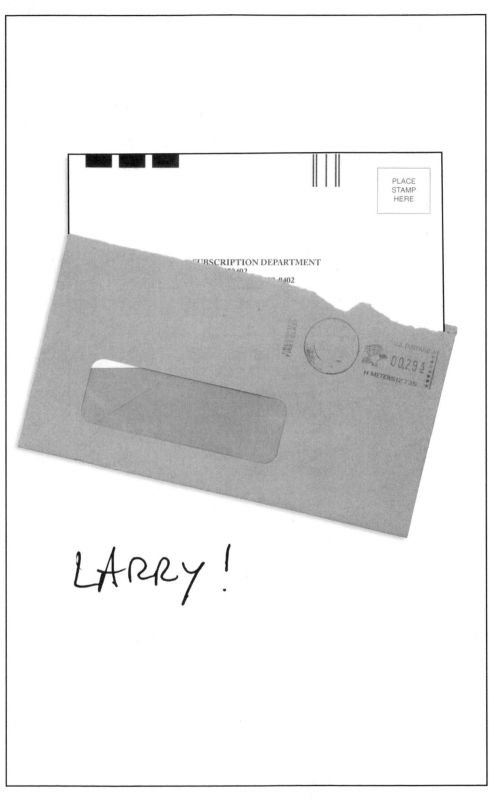

LARRY!

80746
Scott Kablobby
1413 1/2 W Kenneth Rd
Glendale, CA 91201-1478

Now is the time to heal and RENEW.

Dear Scott Kablobby,

Congratulations. You've taken the first step to managing your condition. Your doctor has prescribed PROTONIX. If taken as directed by your doctor, PROTONIX can not only help eliminate acid reflux symptoms, it can heal the erosive damage acid reflux may have caused in your esophagus.

But acid reflux can be a recurring condition that you need to actively manage. So the makers of PROTONIX have developed a program called RENEW to help you do just that.

Discover the science and art of managing acid reflux.
Let the RENEW program show you how.

In clinical trials, the most frequently reported side effects with PROTONIX Delayed-Release Tablets were headache and diarrhea. Relief of your symptoms while on PROTONIX does not exclude the possibility that serious stomach conditions are present. Patients who are allergic to any ingredient of PROTONIX should not take it. **Please see accompanying Prescribing Information.**

Your friends at RENEW

SCOTT KABOBBY
1413 1/2 Kenneth Rd.
#193
Glendale, CA 91201

RENEW ACID REFLEX MEDICINE
PROTONIX
Wyeth Pharmaceuticals
P.O. Box 8299
Philadelphia, PA 19101

Dear Friends at Renew.

You refer to me as Kablobby. My name is Scott Kabobby. You
addressed me as Scott KABLOBBY. There is no L in there.

I noticed you wrote to me that I would have side affects of
headaches and diarrhea. When? If you are indeed my friends at
Renew like you say you are then you will let me know when the
headaches and diarrhea are coming. I use a product called "Head
On" . I applied it to my forehead like the TV commercial says and
it stopped my diarrhea.

I continue to be suspicious of Generalissimo Tazmak. I believe
he has done something with Father Hamooli's prized pig grill.

Sincerely,

Scott Kabobby (NOT Kablobby)

Wyeth Pharmaceuticals
P.O. Box 8299
Philadelphia, PA 19101-8299
484-865-1834

Wyeth

March 6, 2007

Scott Kabobby
1413-1/2 Kenneth Road
#193
Glendale, CA 91201

Dear Mr. Kabobby:

Thank you for your letter regarding the Protonix® Renew Program. Your letter has been forwarded to the program administrators for response.

Please note that Wyeth Pharmaceuticals does not manufacture the product "Head On". We suggest that you speak with the pharmacist at the drug store where you purchased this product for additional information.

For additional information concerning the *Renew* program please call (800) 933-2305, Monday to Friday, 9AM to 5PM EST.

We hope this information is helpful to you. We might also suggest that you discuss any general questions you have with your prescribing physician. Your physician's familiarity with your medical and family history will permit him/her to provide you with that information which is most relevant to your particular situation. Should your physician have any additional questions, please do not hesitate to have him/her contact us.

Sincerely,

Wyeth Medical Communications

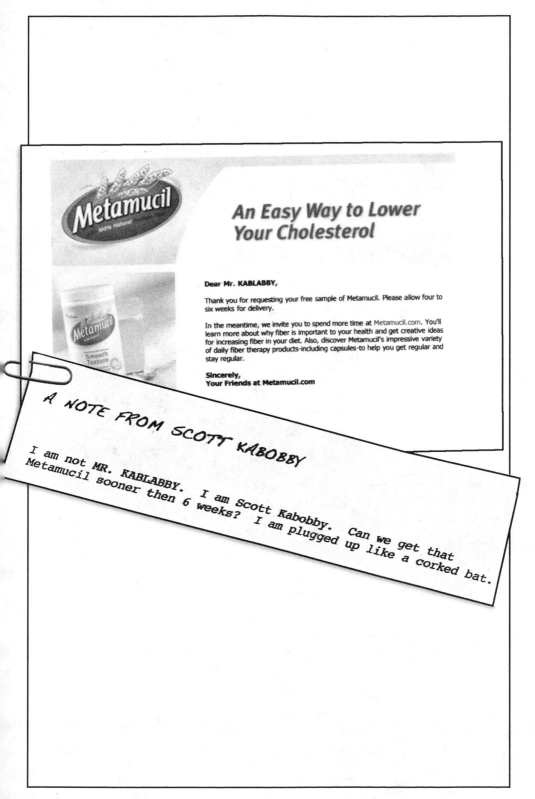

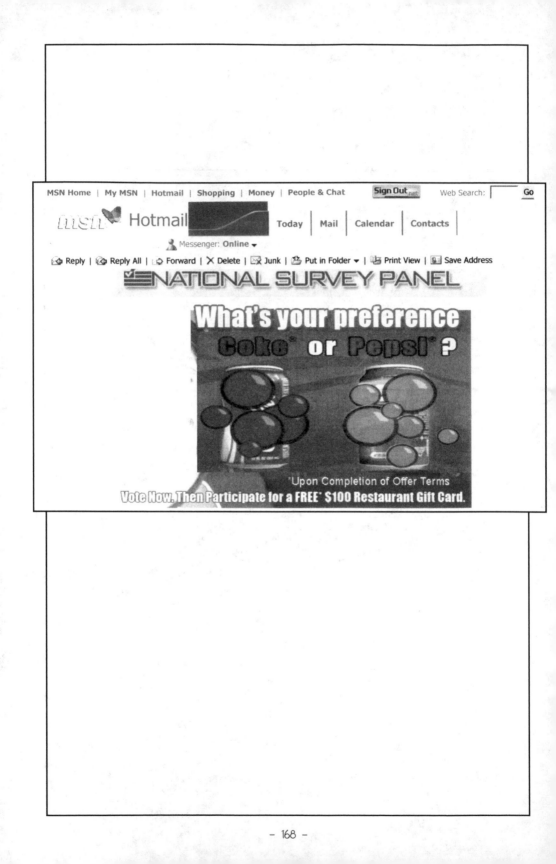

BAHIR KABOBBY
1413 1/2 Kenneth Rd.
#193
Glendale, CA 91201

NATIONAL SURVEY PENAL
COKE OR PEPSI
13900 Jog Rd. #203-251
Delray Beach, FL 33446

Dear Coke Or Pepsi Peoples,

What do I give a pig's hoof about soda preference. There is B.O &
boils everywheres here. I AM BAHIR KABOBBY!!! GRANDFATHER TO
FAMILY!!! HEAR ME LOUD!!!

Tazmak and Laboy are thisclose. In the middle of all this i am
asked my preference for fizzy soft drink? Huh? With what is
going on you expect me to give a flying eggplant? Huh?

SASHIYAMMM!!!! HEELIOMMM!!! I CURSE ALL COKES & PEPSI'S
EVERYWHERE! But for record i like coca cola. It's more of full
bodied soft drink. Hey, coco cola, Do you make Dr. Pepper & 7-Up?
I need to know. I heard Diet Squish is also good drink. And
Wink.

I am living in abandoned homemade jail cell. I long for old
country where i could walk a round in drapes. Not this decrepit
Glendale. My balls itch. (from the swamp back here)

Mazmoosian Respect,

Bahir Kabobby

Coca-Cola
north america

August 6, 2007

Mr. Bahir Kabobby
1413 1/2 Kenneth Rd., No. 193
Glendale, CA 91201

Dear Mr. Kabobby:

Greetings from your friends at The Coca-Cola Company. We are always thrilled to
receive letters from our consumers and appreciate your taking the time to let us know
how much you enjoy our brands.

Did you know that Coca-Cola has been quenching thirsts, such as yours, for over 121
years? We're proud to have earned the title of "World's Favorite Soft Drink," and we owe
it all to loyal consumers such as you. Thank you for your patronage!

Additionally, Dr. Pepper, 7UP, and Wink are not brands of The Coca-Cola Company.

If you have other questions or comments, feel free to write to us again. You may also be
interested in visiting us online at www.coca-cola.com. Best wishes!

Sincerely,

The Coca-Cola Company

Consumer Affairs
Mail Code : DUN
P.O. Box 1734
Atlanta, GA 30301

UNITED STATES POSTAGE
PITNEY BOWES
$ 00.41⁰
02 1A
0004631723   AUG 08 2007
MAILED FROM ZIP CODE 30350

Mr. Bahir Kabobby
1413 1/2 Kenneth Rd., No. 193
Glendale, CA 91201

91201$1478 C008

GENERALISSIMO TAZMAK

HAS STOLEN THE GRILL

Advice and Product Information from the World's Leading Bad Breath Expert

"How To Stop Morning Breath In Less Than 45 Seconds Per Day"

by Dr. Harold Katz
Founder, California Breath Clinics

Finish Reading This Article Online

Dear Scott Kablob,

Since I established the California Breath Clinics back in 1993, **I've encountered just about every kind of breath condition possible....**

From the most offensive situations where you can smell the patients breath from across the room, to those lucky few with breath sweeter than a baby. We've been very fortunate in that we've been able to tackle all types of bad breath, taste disorders, and dry mouth with our TheraBreath line of products.

But, I wanted to share something special with you regarding a category of bad breath and sour/bitter taste common to just about everybody.

First of all, here are some stats.....

Approximately 35% of the world's population has a chronic, noticeable breath condition which usually leads them to seek help from a professional (which may often be incorrect.) This first group has bad breath concerns 24 hours a day, including food odors, taste disorders, dry mouth, and of course "morning breath"....

So what's going on with morning breath?

The thing is, just about EVERYONE has morning breath to one degree or another!

As we sleep throughout the night, our salivary glands slow down (or for some older people - shut down completely) because our brain knows we are not eating. This, combined with the constant flow of air (for those of us who snore or are mouth breathers) over our palate makes for a very DRY environment on the tongue, within our oral cavity and in the throat (the breeding grounds of the anaerobic sulfur-producing bacteria that cause bad breath and taste disorders).

And as I talk about in my article on dry mouth .... this creates an environment that is very conducive for 'morning breath'. (Saliva is nature's way of protecting us from bad breath, because healthy saliva contains high concentrations of oxygen - the natural enemy of anaerobic bacteria.) So if you get morning breath after a good night of sleep - don't worry, you're not alone!

But what most people don't know (and this includes most medical and dental professionals), is that **morning breath is NOT something that you have to live with.**

The key is to find a way to stop the production of VSC's (Volatile Sulfur Compounds) during the night as you are asleep. One way would be to increase the production of saliva within the back of your throat and mouth during the night. But this is very difficult to do - after all, you're asleep! And those of us who are mouth breathers are drying out the back of our throats with each breath that we take throughout the night.

A better way (and easier way) is to stop the production of sulfur compounds by the bacteria that create morning breath...

Warmest Regards,

Dr. Harold Katz

-Harold Katz, DDS

SCOTT KABOBBY
1413 1/2 Kenneth Rd.
#193
Glendale, CA 91201

DR. HAROLD KATZ
CALIFORNIA BREATH CLINICS
750 N. Highland Ave
Los Angeles, CA 90038

Dear Dr. Katz.

I am Scott Kabobby. Not Scott Kablob. You addressed me as Scott Kablob in your mail to me. But that's OK I am dealing with alot on my plate now. I have that under control as long as there's medication under my swollen infected tongue.

I have massive cigarette breath. I smoke over 1,000 cigarettes a day. Only L&M. Why L&M? I like the cool taste of L&M and the fresh crisp feel of a good cigarette. It's the taste to start with and the taste to stay with.

My mouth is a dark weird color and my gums are speckled like cheap terrazzo tile in a public mens room. I smell like cowboy shorts. So my question to you is:

HOW DO I AVOID NASTY MORNING BREATH?

Now to my family: The big news is that it has been found out that Generalissimo Tazmak has stolen my dad Hamooli's grill. Not Grandfather Bahir as suspected. Grandfather Bahir is innocent. When Grandfather Bahir found this out - after being blamed for 63 days straight and called a miserable thief - he festered. What is he up to? Who can blame him. My back itches from a mismarked ointment. I may have caught something from a bad Theme Park ride. Are cooties still around? I have night sweats on my face. It's good to have you in my life, Dr. Katz. Together we will have me smelling Sweeeet! My cough is so bad that yesterday I phlemed up somebody elses spool. Is that bad?

With respect for bad breath,

Razi "Scott" Hamooli

The California Breath Clinics
750 N. Highland Ave.
Los Angeles, CA 90038

Hi Scott Kablob,

I hope you're having a terrific July! Here is a question that keeps popping up on
THERABREATH.COM during hot summer weather:

Dear Dr. Katz: How do I avoid nasty morning breath?

It's really very easy to avoid most types of morning breath with our **TheraBreath Oral Rinse**
and **Toothpaste**. But here is a little trick that really works for problem breath.

1. Right before bedtime, use your TheraBreath Oral Rinse and Toothpaste as directed, **making
sure to coat your tongue with toothpaste as part of the process.**
2. After your regular TheraBreath routine, **place 1-2 TheraBreath FreshStrips directly on
the back of your tongue.**
3. Now go to bed and wake up without nasty morning breath! That's all there is to it.
At night when you sleep, the **Anaerobic Sulfur-Producing Bacteria** that are responsible for
awful breath have a field day in your mouth because oxygen-rich saliva is not being produced.
The slow dissolving action of our patented, pharmaceutical-grade **TheraBreath FreshStrips**
continues to work through the night, controlling anaerobic sulfur-producing bacteria that live in
your mouth and cause unpleasant morning breath. The combination of TheraBreath Rinse,
Toothpaste, and FreshStrips is the closest thing to mimicking the anti-bacterial properties of
healthy saliva.

Now, even better news: I really want you to try the strips out for yourself to see what a
difference they make. I am so sure you will love this product, I am enclosing a coupon for
$1.50 OFF a pack of 24 TheraBreath FreshStrips good at any store that carries them.

Do you have more questions about morning breath?
If you have any specific questions about oral care, don't hesitate to ask me. That's why I'm here.

Enjoy the wonderful weather!

Dr. Harold Katz, DDS

PS: The FreshStrips have been a huge hit with the Celebrity clients in my Beverly Hills practice. In
fact, some very famous names now **require TheraBreath FreshStrips** in their contract if
they have to do a kissing scene. These folks could chose any product line they want, and they
chose TheraBreath. To me there is no better endorsement than that.

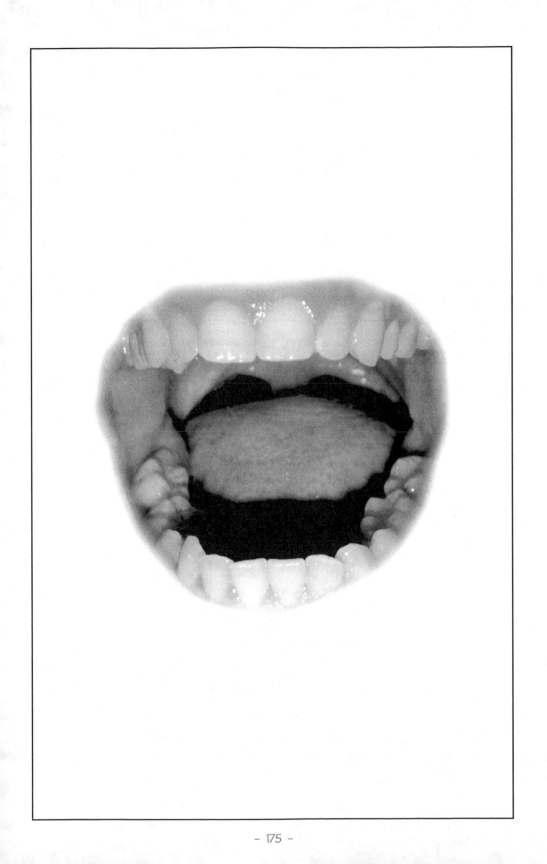

Sent :	Wednesday, November 22, 2006 9:08 AM
To :	Bahir Kabobby
Subject :	Motel 6

Good Day Mr. Kabobby,

I have recently received your email request for information regarding development in British Columbia for Motel 6.
Your request did not include a phone number so I could speak with you directly.
I would be pleased to forward you an information package but could you please let me know 1) if there is a particular area of interest in the province, 2) if you already have a site, 3) the size of facility, number of rooms, you are considering and 4) the amount of equity you have to invest.

Thank you for your interest as I look forward to hearing from you.

Realstar Hospitality
1221 Camas Crt.
Victoria, BC

BAHIR KABOBBY
1413 1/2 Kenneth Rd.
#193
Glendale, CA 91201

Motel Person
Director Of Deveolpment
Motel Chain
Voctorias, BC
V8X 4R1

Dear Motel Person of Motel 6:

I am vindicated! It is now known that I DID NOT STEAL HAMOOLI'S
GRILL! I knew it, Judge Joe Brown knew it, yet none of my
stinking relatives knew it. But did i do it? NO! I AM
GRANDFATHER BAHIR!! LEADER OF FAMILY!!! HEAR ME LOUD!!!

Who did it? That miserable Generalissimo Tazmak. Who is now
living with Coco LaBoy and they are up to something. What, I do
not know.

You asked me how many rooms i am considering. How many do you
have? Ha Ha Ha!! I need as many rooms as i can get. I am
cramped. Let's work together on getting me motel room, Mr. Motel
Leader of Motel 6 chain.   Whatever happened to Motels 1-5? Was
there a problem? or just working it out?

With respect for honesty,

Bahir Kabobby

To : Bahir Kabobby

Subject : Motel 6

Good day mr. Kabobby,

I have today received your letter and I will be pleased to forward you an
information package and address your questions but please confirm back to me by
return email that your mailing address is: 1413 1/2 Kenneth Rd. #193., Glendale,
CA, 91201. If this is not correct please forward correct mailing address.

I look forward to hearing from you.

Realstar Hospitality
1221 Camas Crt.
Victoria, BC

BAHIR KABOBBY
1413 1/2 Kenneth Rd.
#193
Glendale, CA 91201

Motel Person
Director Of Deveolpment
Motel Chain
Voctorias, BC
V8X 4R1

Dear Motel Person of Motel 6:

I am confirming back to you address: 1413 1/2 Kenneth Rd. #193
(refrigerator carton) Glendale, CA 91201. It is stinking pit back
here. I have disease on top of foot.

Let's discuss Motel 6 room. I need! New investors may include:
Generalissimo Tazmak & his associate Coco LaBoy. (who I believe i
caught foot disease from) Geela Kabobby no longer investor due to
Reader's Digest Magazine situation.

Thanking you for response in Motel talks. Look at my foot if you
are ever in town.

Respect for peoples:

Bahir Kobobby

MY Home

To :   Bahir Kabobby

Subject :   Motel 6

I received your letter and when you actually have a Canadian market area and
site you are interested in and have your investor situation straightened out,
you can call me then. I wish you luck in your endeavours.

Realstar Hospitality
1221 Camas Crt.
Victoria, BC

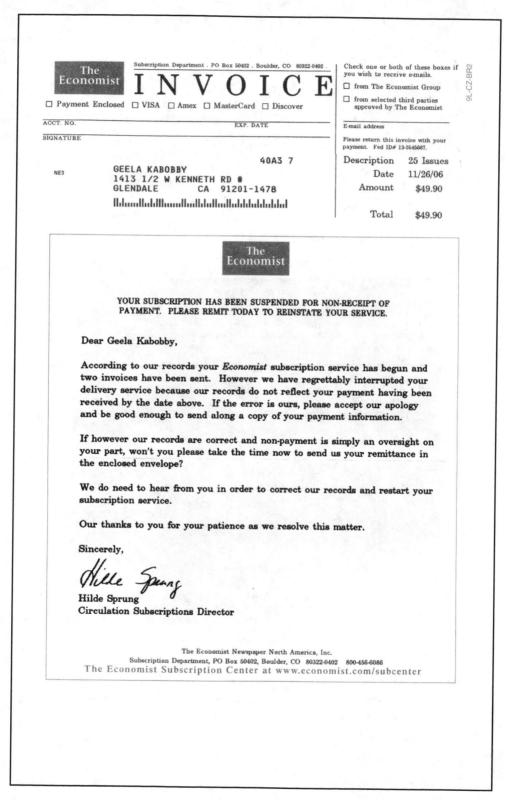

The Economist

Subscription Department . PO Box 50402 . Boulder, CO 80322-0402 .

INVOICE

☐ Payment Enclosed ☐ VISA ☐ Amex ☐ MasterCard ☐ Discover

Check one or both of these boxes if you wish to receive e-mails.

☐ from The Economist Group

☐ from selected third parties
  approved by The Economist

9L-CZ-BR2

ACCT. NO.   EXP. DATE

SIGNATURE

E-mail address

Please return this invoice with your payment. Fed ID# 13-3545667.

NE3

40A3 7

GEELA KABOBBY
1413 1/2 W KENNETH RD #
GLENDALE   CA   91201-1478

Description	25 Issues
Date	11/26/06
Amount	$49.90
Total	$49.90

The Economist

YOUR SUBSCRIPTION HAS BEEN SUSPENDED FOR NON-RECEIPT OF PAYMENT. PLEASE REMIT TODAY TO REINSTATE YOUR SERVICE.

Dear Geela Kabobby,

According to our records your *Economist* subscription service has begun and two invoices have been sent. However we have regrettably interrupted your delivery service because our records do not reflect your payment having been received by the date above. If the error is ours, please accept our apology and be good enough to send along a copy of your payment information.

If however our records are correct and non-payment is simply an oversight on your part, won't you please take the time now to send us your remittance in the enclosed envelope?

We do need to hear from you in order to correct our records and restart your subscription service.

Our thanks to you for your patience as we resolve this matter.

Sincerely,

Hilde Sprung
Circulation Subscriptions Director

The Economist Newspaper North America, Inc.
Subscription Department, PO Box 50402, Boulder, CO 80322-0402   800-456-6086
The Economist Subscription Center at www.economist.com/subcenter

GEELA KABOBBY
1413 1/2 Kenneth Rd.
#193
Glendale, CA 91201

THE ECONOMIST MAGAZINE
P.O. Box 50402
Boulder, Colorodo
80322-0402

Dear Economist:

Re: Your subscription suspension to me. I am sad. Economist was
my only pleasure. I enjoyed reading your business & political
analysis.

What can we do? I have no money. It was sold on Ebay. When will
my next issue of Econimynist arrive? I am waiting.

With Respect For Economist and their subscriptions,

Geela Kabobby
Sad (3rd notice of sadness)

GEELA KABOBBY
1413 1/2 Kenneth Rd.
#193
Glendale, CA 91201

THE ECONOMIST MAGAZINE
P.O. Box 50402
Boulder, Colorodo
80322-0402

Dear Economist:

Re: my subscription overdue. Good news! I am involved in Motel 5 deal that will allow me to pay off $49.90 once Mr. Motel 5 gets me many rooms to rent out. Bahir Kabobby taking care of all details. Coco Laboy has pledged help in this matter. His sister has herpes. Look at Bahir's foot when you are in town.

I hope this answers ALL questions concerning my subscription.

Respectfully,

Geela Kabobby

TheraBreath

Advice and Product Information from the World's Leading Bad Breath Expert

News and Information from the *California Breath Clinics*

"Are You Doing the Basics?"

by Dr. Harold Katz
Founder, California Breath Clinics

Finish Reading This Article Online

Dear Scott Kablob,

Every single day at The California Breath Clinics, we receive hundreds of emails from people who want help and relief from bad breath, dry mouth, or lousy tastes. These emails usually range in assortment from '**Where do I start?**' to '**How does this Work?**' to '**HELP ME!**'

But some of the most distressing emails I read are those that start out like this: '*Dr. Katz, I bought your power drops, and tried them today but I still have bad breath. I'm brushing with Colgate and rinsing with Listerine - why do I still have bad breath?*'

Let me put it another way.....

When you go to work in the morning, every once in a while you might spend some extra time and invest in a nice hat, maybe a tie, or a nice new pair of shoes. But if you forget to put on a blouse/shirt and pants, you'd look pretty funny, and that nice new pair of shoes or hat wouldn't do much good!

I can't stress it enough - you've GOT to be doing the basics!

More pressure

In my world, the basics are using TheraBreath toothgel, Oral Rinse, and a tongue scraper **at least twice daily.** If you have bad breath, it's NOT enough to use regular commercial toothpaste and mouthwash, because these products actually dry out your mouth. You MUST be using an oxygenating toothpaste and a mouthwash that does not contain alcohol (to prevent dry mouth).

Once you're doing the basics, only then will you find relief by using a breath spray or power drops. Those items are SUPPLEMENTS, not replacements.

So before you ask me what you're doing wrong, PLEASE make sure you are doing the basics below.

1. Scrape your tongue gently with a dry tongue scraper to remove the mucous layer.
2. Put some TheraBreath toothgel on the tongue scraper and apply it evenly to the back of your tongue.
3. Let the toothgel sit on your tongue while you are brushing your teeth. Brush thoroughly for 60 seconds.
4. When you are done brushing, spit out, but DO NOT rinse with water. Rinse with 1-2 capfuls of TheraBreath Oral Rinse for 60 seconds.

When you order 'The Basics' you can receive a free TheraBreath powerdrops and free UPS Ground Shipping!

Warmest Regards,

Dr. Harold Katz

-Harold Katz, DDS

DR. HAROLD KATZ
CALIFORNIA BREATH CLINICS
750 N. Highland Ave
Los Angeles, CA 90038

Dear Dr. Katz.

You still refer to be as Kablob. I am Scott Kabobby. Not Scott
KABLOB. You addressed me again as Scott Kablob in your mail to
me. But that's OK I am dealing with alot on my plate now. So
this is just one more thing.

I AM DOING THE BASICS. JUST LIKE YOU WROTE ME!!! What are your
Power Drops you refer to? I use a tongue scraper every 3 minutes.
I scraped a layer of tongue off my tongue and you know what I
found under there. More tongue (with more bad breath)

My mother, Geela, is insulted that Coco LaBoy has become engaged
to Generalissimo Tazmak. What is going on back here??? The whole
thing is just toooo weird. That problem is worse then my breath
or feet or facial blushing or moles or random hairs or acid
reflux, or elongated nipples, or sploongy. THAT is a sick
relationship, Dr. Katz. Let's talk about that, shall we???   I
have to go now. My ointment on my feet is wearing off and i have
diarrhea from TOO much of that Head On wax.

Tongue Scraper Guy,

Scott Kabobby (NOT Kablob)

370 South Fairfax Ave.
Los Angeles, CA 90036

Dear Scott Kablob,

Recent research has uncovered a startling new discovery about the mouthwash you are probably using. Did you know that over 90% of the mouthwash that is commercially available contains an acid level comparable to that of household vinegar?   *NO!*

Can you imagine rinsing and gargling with vinegar? I don't even have to tell you what that would taste like, but think for a second what it can do to your teeth!

The enamel on your teeth is one of the hardest substances that your body can produce. But acid is one of the most corrosive substances in nature. The study below which was completed in April of 2001 discovered that rinsing your mouth with a mouthwash that contains a high concentration of acid causes a drastic increase in enamel loss.

And enamel loss has a direct correlation to sensitivity in teeth - **people with less enamel complained of much greater sensitivity in their teeth to hot and cold.**

As you can see from the chart online - almost all commercially available **mouthwashes** have a highly acidic environment. But ThoraBreath **is actually an 'antacid' mouthwash!**

Moral of the Story: **Use a Non-Acidic Mouthwash.**

Warmest Regards,

-Harold Katz, DDS

SCOTT KABOBBY
1413 1/2 Kenneth Rd.
#193
Glendale, CA 91201

DR. HAROLD KATZ
CALIFORNIA BREATH CLINICS
750 N. Highland Ave
Los Angeles, CA 90038

Dear Dr. Katz.

Once again, you still refer to be as Kablob. I am Scott Kabobby. Not Scott Kablob. I must tell you once more...You addressed me again as Scott Kablob in your mail to me. (mentioned this before. OK?) But that's FINE I am dealing with a lot on my plate now. So this is just one more thing.

Last time i wrote you, you asked me to do the basics. Now you want me to use a non acidic mouthwash. And no - I can't imagine rinsing and gargling with vinegar. Why do you ask??? And why do you keep calling me Kablob? It's really bothering me now. I have asked you NICELY not to refer to me as Kablob.

Coco Laboy hinted that Generalissimo Tazmak may know where Hamooli's grill is. Shouldn't he tell us???

I think my gums are bleeding. is that bad?

Mouthwash Vinegar Guy,

Scott Kabobby (NOT Kablob!)

Hello Scott Kablob,

It's true - there have been numerous scientific studies which prove beyond a shadow of a doubt that <u>**Bleeding Gums (and gum disease in general) can cause heart disease, stroke, and even can be responsible for premature births and low birth weight babies in pregnant women!**</u>

Fortunately Scott Kablob, there is now something you can do about it. I've prepared a new article for you called "Oral Care Secrets", and you can get it for fr~ee, right now! Just click below:

Grab Your Complimentary Copy of
' Oral Care Secrets: Why Bleeding Gums May Shorten Your Life!'

Warmest Regards,

Dr. Harold Katz

-Harold Katz, DDS

<u>**This Email Has Been Sent From:**</u>
The California Breath Clinics
750 N. Highland Ave.
Los Angeles, CA 90038
800.97.FRESH or 323.993.8320

P.S. I've also prepared a nice surprise especially for you, Scott Kablob because you allow me to talk with you by email. Make sure to look for the big green button on the page above!

To stop receiving future emails from Dr. Katz just go to
http://www.therabreath.com/emailoptions.asp

SCOTT KABOBBY
1413 1/2 Kenneth Rd.
#193
Glendale, CA 91201

DR. HAROLD KATZ
CALIFORNIA BREATH CLINICS
750 N. Highland Ave
Los Angeles, CA 90038

Dear Dr. Katz.

Are you even listening to me??? At all??? I write to you with specific questions and get weird answers back. MY MOUTH SMELLS LIKE THE CARPET FROM AN INDIAN CASINO. I currently smoke 2,000 cigarettes a day. (Only L & M's. Why L & M? I like the cool taste of L & M and the fresh crisp feel of a good cigarette. It's the taste to start with and the taste to stay with.)

I DID NOT ask you about bleeding gums. Yet you write me about bleeding gums. I can't imagine what my "nice surprise" is that you mention in your last letter to me.

I have followed all your advice. I have scraped my tongue until it is raw. I looked at it yesterday and it is see through now. I took 2 layers of tongue off. All I see under there are veins and wires. I gargle with vinegar like you say.

Is there anyone else out there that has a breath problem?

I know you are a great dentist. I have heard from others that you are. I JUST NEED HELP. MY MOUTH SMELLS LIKE GRANDMA PANTIES.

Help Me. Please.

Scott Kablob (I am giving up and calling myself this now)

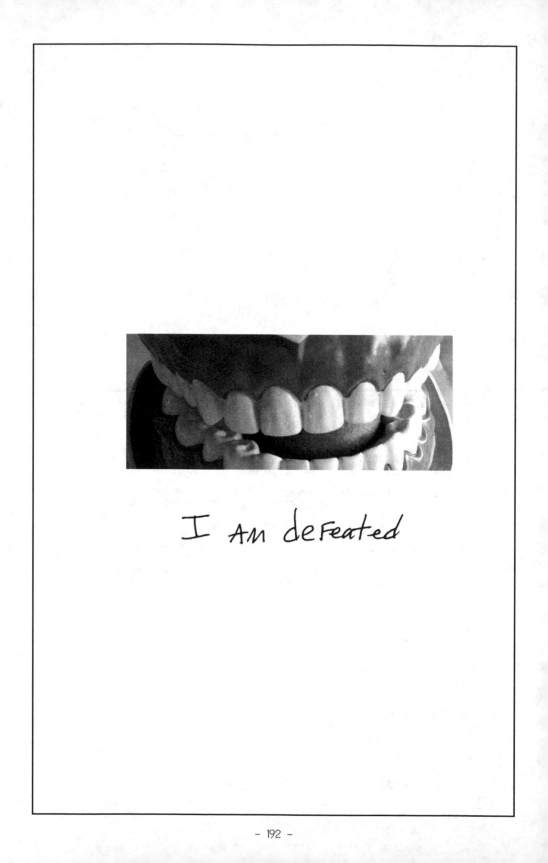

I Am deFeated

California Breath Clinics
750 N. Highland Ave.
Los Angeles, CA 90038

Hello Scott Kablob,

Dr. Katz is one of the top experts in the world on the topic of bad breath and halitosis. Over the last 10 years he has personally helped thousands of patients, and tens of thousands more have come through his clinics and been helped by his knowledge.

I know because I am one of them - I don't remember the last time someone offered me a piece of gum or a mint, and it's a wonderful feeling.

Dr. Katz takes great pride in running the office just like a "dentist office", so if you have ANY questions at all, don't hesitate to let us know. Our contact information is:

patientcare@drkatz.com
OR(888) FRESH-88 or (323) 993-8320

I hope you learn something from your reading - those who have bad breath know that this can be a VERY demoralizing problem to deal with, however it is helpful to know that an end is within your grasp.

Warmest Regards,

Patient Care
California Breath Clinics

INVEST WITH CONFIDENCE

November 6, 2006

Dear Hamooli Kabobby:

At T. Rowe Price, we take a fundamental, risk-aware approach to investing. It has proven successful for over 65 years and has helped thousands of individuals reach their long-term savings goals.

Managed for growth. Managed to reduce risk.

The **T. Rowe Price Capital Appreciation Fund** has a record of solid, proven performance. It's appropriate for investors looking for a fund that focuses on reducing risk as much as maximizing gains. The fund employs a value strategy, investing in well-established U.S. companies whose future earnings T. Rowe Price believes to be undervalued by the current market. Because the fund invests in large, well-established companies with proven track records, the fund can benefit from gains during bull markets, as well as offer some cushion during market corrections. The fund may also invest in a selection of bonds in an attempt to preserve assets. Specific to a value-oriented strategy, there is the possibility that the undervalued stocks in which the fund invests may actually be appropriately priced or may have an intrinsic value that is not recognized by the market for a long time, if at all.

It's easy to get started.

Investing in the fund is easy—*simply complete the Open an Account Form and return it with your check. If you want to transfer assets currently invested at another firm, also fill out the enclosed Transfer of Non-retirement Assets Form and return it. Enclosed is a profile; if you would like to receive a prospectus, please call 1-800-821-2331. The profile and prospectus include investment objectives, risks, fees, expenses, and other information that you should read and consider carefully before investing.*

If you have more questions about the Capital Appreciation Fund or any of our 90 no-load mutual funds, visit us at **troweprice.com/start**, or call our Investment Guidance Specialists at **1-800-821-2331**.

For more in-depth assistance in choosing a fund, ask our Investment Guidance Specialists. They can help you decide if a particular fund is right for you and even offer guidance on your entire portfolio.

Sincerely,

Edward C. Bernard

Edward C. Bernard
President
T. Rowe Price Investment Services, Inc.

HAMOOLI KABOBBY
1413 1/2 Kenneth Rd.
#193
Glendale, CA 91201

EDWARD C. BERNARD
T ROWE PRICE PEOPLES
PO Box 17630
Baltimore, MD 21297-1630

Dear Edward Bernard.

I like peoples with 2 first names. You have Edward and Bernard.
In my country I once knew man with 2 first names: Hasi & Yasnati.
So you two have much in commons. Now down to T Rowe Price. Which
is 2 last names. Rowe and Price. In my country i once knew mans
with 2 last names. Lashee & Feezeelo. And peoples were mistaking
them for shoe names. (do you have Feezeelo in size 9? Ha Ha Ha)
So he and your company have much in common.

Let me be candid with you, Bernard C. Edwards -- it is now widely
known now that: GENERALISSIMO TAZMAK HAS STOLEN MY GRILL!!!

We have investigated and found out that much. All along i blamed
my own grandfather. Listen to me, I must be up front and candid
with you. GENERALISSIMO TAZMAK TOOK GRILL! HE STOLE IT. HE IS
GUM INFECTED TONGUE SCRAPING S.O.B. THAT SHOULD HAVE FLEA IN HIS
HAIR AND MORE WHITE COATING ON HIS TONGUE. (Like my son, Scott.)
I CURSE HIS EYEBALL!!

Am i making sense, Bernie? Tazmak now Living in new egg box with
Coco LaBoy. I am getting family together and trying to demote him
down a rank to Colonel but it is hard. There is much paperwork
needed and that is where you fit in. T Rowe Price can generate
lot of paperwork for me. I see the amount of mail you send me
every day. When do we start? How do we do it? I look forward to
more paperwork from you and reduction in rank of the
Generalissimo.

Shwarmi is trying to meet Internet peoples under name PEPPER SPRAY
IN FACE. Ha! What peoples would contact madman with that name?
Huh, Bernards?

With respect for your investment mail,

Hamooli Kabobby

Hello, PEPPERSPRAYINFACE!
You have requested to receive Absolute Agency Top Members.

Don't wait for love to find you, contact everyone you like by joining as Privileged Member.
Please take a look at the previews below.
To view member's complete profile, just press photo or name:

Dear PEPPERSPRAYINFACE,
Please press here to activate Your Profile.

You have successfully registered with AbsoluteAgency.com, world's
leading Matchmaking Service! We offer easy and effective way to
discover new friends, start dating or meet your potential bride... It's
Fast!

Your profile ID:
Your password:

You can use this information to update personal information.
Press to find how other members will see your ad.

Start new relationship in two easy steps.

Hello, PEPPERSPRAYINFACE!
Apply for 5 days privileged membership only for $2.95 today and
get in contact with any member of AbsoluteAgency.com!
Privileged membership will give you ability to access all paid
services!

You can send Unlimited number of emails, whisper and flirt in private chat room, and finally, after 5 days, we
will extend your privileged membership at discounted rate!

MEET
YOUR
DATE
Click
here
Register as
Privileged Member and Send mail

24/7 live Chat room
Full Membership have several privileges
ENTER

Stop Waiting &
START DATING TODAY!

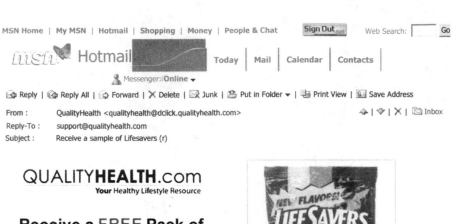

Snacks that can help with dental health

Snacks like gum or hard candies help promote healthy teeth. The saliva created by chewing or sucking on a snack helps clean your teeth and remove food leftover from eating. Of course, it's always best to choose sugar free gum and candies to promote good eating habits and minimize sugar intake.

TAHINI KABOBBY
1413 1/2 Kenneth Rd.
#193
Glendale, CA 91201

LIFESAVERS
QUALITY HEALTH
510 Thornall St 130
Edison, NJ 08837

Dear Free Pack Of Lifesavers.

Wow! Lifesavers! Cool! Free Pack. Aw Yea! Ba dink a dink! da
bomb! 5 Flavors! Booty do! Boo Yah! Cracalakin' deelicious
bongo beatin life savers dawwwwwggg!

Be Easy, Lifesavers

Tahini Kabobby

cool wit dat

Wm. **WRIGLEY** *Jr. Company*

P.O. BOX 3900
PEORIA, ILLINOIS 61612
Telephone: 1-800-WRIGLEY

March 2, 2007

Tahini Kabobby
1413 1/2 W Kenneth Rd
Glendale CA 91201-1478

Dear Tahini,

Thank you for contacting the Wrigley Company to request information. We sincerely appreciate your interest in our Company and brands.

You'll be happy to know that our researchers are constantly working on new flavors to add to our product lineup, and it's possible that, in the future, we'll introduce additional flavors of Life Savers candies. We hope you will keep an eye out for our new products, try them when they come out and let us know what you think.

It's hard to believe that a great tasting product like chewing gum has important dental benefits, but it's true! Saliva
is your body's natural defense against tooth decay. It contains buffering agents that help neutralize the acid. When you chew gum, the acid is neutralized after 20 minutes of chewing. That's because gum chewing stimulates salivation at three times the normal rate.

We hope this information has been helpful. If you have any additional questions or comments please feel free to contact us at 1-800-WRIGLEY Monday through Friday from 8:30 a.m. to 5:00 p.m. CST.

Sincerely,

Consumer Affairs Representative

```
                                        HAMOOLI KABOBBY
                                        1413 1/2 Kenneth Rd.
                                        #193
                                        Glendale, CA 91201




CREDIT LINE FOR U
Big Hip
888 Veterans Memorial Highway
Hauppauge, NY 11788




Dear Mummy Cash.

Where is it?  I need it now.  How do I get it?  The money.
($1500.00 - or whatever that is Shabazzi)




Thank you,
```

Hamooli Kabobby (signature)

Hamooli Kabobby

Scott Kabooby:
Thank you in advance for trying Netflix, the no-hassle way to rent DVDs.

Enclosed is everything you need to get started... including a coupon for FREE DVD RENTALS!

Dear Scott,

You're all set to go!

Just redeem the coupon above (instructions are on back). In about one business day, you'll get your first selections in our bright red Netflix envelopes. Keep them as long as you want, then return them in the postage-free envelope provided. Your next movies will then arrive a couple of days later. It's easy. It's fun. And remember:

- **PRESSURE-FREE:** There's no rush to return DVDs. No running to the store before closing. No late fees.
- **HASSLE-FREE:** DVDs are delivered to you in about one business day.
- **SHIPPING IS FREE:** Both Ways – return each movie in its prepaid return mailer.
- **PLANS FOR EVERYONE**, from only 4^{99} a month.

Redeem your coupon now. Enjoy your free rentals. And try the no-hassle, no-limit way to rent DVDs.

Sincerely,

Neve Savage

Neve Savage,
Vice President

P.S. Can't think of movies off the top of your head? We've enclosed the Netflix TOP 200 to give you some ideas. We've also included a FREE New Release Calendar that tells you what's coming in the months ahead. You can actually put them in your Netflix queue now and get them when they become available. Go to www.netflix.com/specialoffer to get even more ideas and to redeem your coupon now.

① Over **70,000 Titles**

Create your list of DVDs online.

② Free delivery in about **1 Business Day**

We rush you DVDs from your list.

③ NO LATE FEES

Keep each DVD as long as you want.

④ Prepaid **return envelopes**

Return a movie to get a new one from your list

CU0158208-30010158230

SCOTT KABOBBY
1413 1/2 Kenneth Rd.
#193
Glendale, CA 91201

NETFLIX
Lansdale, PA

Dear Netflix.

I AM NOT SCOTT KABOOBY!!! You addressed me as Scott Kabooby. My
name is Kabobby. NOT Kabooby. Please correct this in your mail
data base.

Of course i want to rent DVD's. Who wouldn't? But I am a mess,
Netflix. I can only watch as i deteriorate. I cannot watch
movies? My family hates me. They think I am a lox.

Does netflix have a foot department? I wanted some foot items.
Can someone assist me? I may have hammertoe.

Should i get the total foot care kit? Or just the partial foot
care kit, Netflix? YOU WOULD KNOW!!! Please get back to me on
my twisted toes. While i like movies and will rent as many as you
have, if you can help my decrepit feet i will rent dvd's from you.

Netflix is highly recommended in the dvd area. I saw a bird
siting on one of your red envelopes inside a mailbox and it was
happy.

Thank you,

Razi "Scott" Kabobby

GRANDFATHER BAHIR says...
HAMOOLI -- YOU PIECE OF DECREPID PESTO. I DO NOT TAKE YOUR GRILL!!! ENJOY THIS
YOU BELZARRIAN C#CKSU*K&R!!! BAHIR

Afghan Beef Raviolis (Mantwo)

Submitted By:
★★★★★ Read Reviews (3) | Rate/Review this recipe

Prep Time: 45
Minutes
Cook Time: 1
Hour 25 Minutes
Ready In: 2
Hours 10
Minutes
Yields:
4 servings

"Popular at a well-known Afghan restaurant nearby, this dish uses wontons to create
delicious beef-, bean- and spice-filled raviolis with an Afghani twist."

Be the first to
submit a photo
for this recipe

INGREDIENTS:

3/4 cup plain yogurt
1 teaspoon chopped fresh mint leaves
2 cloves garlic, crushed

1 pound ground beef
1 1/2 cups chopped onion
1 cup water
1 carrot, grated
3/4 teaspoon salt
1 teaspoon ground black pepper
1 1/2 teaspoons ground coriander

GRANDFATHER BAHIR THROWS A RAVIOLI POOP INSIDE A DENNYS

If you have a bladder control problem, **don't worry,** it may be a treatable condition

Dear Bahir Kabobby,

I understand what living with a bladder control problem is like. I have seen firsthand what my patients go through every day.

I know it's not just the symptoms of overactive bladder (OAB) that make your life so difficult:
- The strong, sudden urges to urinate
- Often going more than 8 times in 24 hours, which may include waking up at night to go
- Wetting accidents (for some people)

You also worry about making it to the bathroom in time. Or keeping the problem to yourself. When you think about it, a condition like OAB can add a lot of stress to your life!

So why do people put up with OAB? A lot of people think it's part of aging. But OAB is not normal at any age. And there's a proven treatment called DETROL LA that may help your symptoms. It helps calm the bladder muscle that causes those sudden urges to go. One pill a day can provide all day, all night relief.* It's the #1 prescribed brand of OAB medicine. And DETROL LA is covered by most health plans.

Please take the next step. Ask your doctor if DETROL LA can help you.

The enclosed booklet will tell you some of the causes of OAB and how DETROL LA may help. Take a few minutes to look it over. Then follow the "Talking to Your Doctor" guide. It has really important info to share with your doctor. Plus, ideas on how to make your appointment go smoothly.

Sincerely,

Tamara Bavendam

Tamara Bavendam, MD
Medical Director

If you don't want to learn or receive more information about DETROL LA, call 1-888-735-3208. We'll take you off our DETROL LA mailing list.

If you have certain stomach problems, glaucoma, or trouble getting urine to pass, you shouldn't take DETROL LA. The most common side effects are dry mouth, headache, constipation and abdominal pain. DETROL LA, like all medicines, has benefits and risks. There may be other options. Ask your doctor if DETROL LA is right for you.

*Individual results may vary.

Please see accompanying important product information.

Detrol LA
tolterodine tartrate
extended release capsules

BAHIR KABOBBY
1413 1/2 Kenneth Rd.
#193
Glendale, CA 91201

Medical Dept.
DETROL BLADDER CONTROL PEOPLES
PFIZER
235 E 42 st
NY, NY 10017

Dear Medical Dept.

I once knew dentist named Tom Barverdim. Is that your department?
How did you know i had bladder control problem? My egg crate
smells like cat pound. I am tired of stink back here. It smell
better in bus station after Urine Festival.

I am sad, sad man. I am admitting:: I threw a poop inside a
Dennys on Kenneth Rd. It was a Ravioli Poop, red and brown and I
mixed it up in my new fig crate while I watched Judge Joe Brown
rule on rake. Yaggi watched me mix it up. His cousin bought some
medicated socks today in Razastan and showed them to us on his
cell phone. I am sorry for my behavior. But what can I do,
Dexatrol?

I noticed your most common side effects are dry mouth, headache,
constipation, and abdominal pain. Hey, that is pretty good
Saturday night for me. I WOULD THROW RAVIOLI POOP AGAIN IF I HAD
THE CHANCE!!!

With respect for Detrol and ravioli (but not poop),

Bahir Kabobby

Detrol LA

tolterodine tartrate
extended release capsules

**********AUTO**MIXED AADC 640
2091454914 187
Bahir Kabobby
1413 1/2 W Kenneth Rd # 193
Glendale, CA 91201-1478
Il.l......ll.l.lll......ll...ll.l.ll...ll.l.l.l..l.l.l.l

Don't worry, talking to your doctor about
your overactive bladder can be easy.

Because now you have the right tools.

Dear Bahir Kabobby,

Recently, you contacted us about your overactive bladder. We outlined 3 steps that may help you
find relief. They are: be aware of your symptoms, keep a bladder diary and tell your doctor how your
symptoms make you feel.

If you have not talked to your doctor yet, we've enclosed these tools to help you get started:

- A quiz that can help you note the things in life your bladder control problem has kept you
  from enjoying
- A second copy of our helpful "Talking to Your Doctor" guide. Fill it out and share it with
  your doctor

The sooner you talk to your doctor, the sooner you can feel better and worry less about your bladder
control problem.

Regards,

Tamara Bavendam

Tamara Bavendam, MD
Medical Director

Important Safety Information. If you have certain types of stomach problems, glaucoma or if you have
trouble getting urine to pass, you shouldn't take DETROL LA. The most common side effects are dry
mouth, headache, constipation, and abdominal pain.

DETROL LA, like all medicines, has risks and benefits. There may be other options. Ask your doctor if
DETROL LA is right for you.

If you don't want to learn or receive more information about DETROL LA, call 1-888-735-3208.
We'll take you off our DETROL LA mailing list.

Uninsured? Need help paying for medicine? Pfizer has programs that can help,
no matter your age or income. You may even qualify for free Pfizer medicines.
Call 1-866-706-2400. Or visit www.pfizerhelpfulanswers.com.

helpful answers

Please see accompanying important product information.
DIKIT214

DD260540A   ©2006 Pfizer Inc.   All rights reserved.   Printed in USA/June 2006   **Pfizer** U.S. Pharmaceuticals   10% TOTAL RECOVERED FIBER

BAHIR KABOBBY
1413 1/2 Kenneth Rd.
#193
Glendale, CA 91201

Medical Dept.
DETROL BLADDER CONTROL PEOPLES
PFIZER
235 E 42 st
NY, NY 10017

Dear Medical Dept:

Thank you for personal letter you sent me regarding my bladder
problem. I told you i threw poop in a Dennys and you did not
judge me. You just sent me reply telling me to keep bladder diary
which I took your advice and did. Here is 1st entry in diary.
Tell me how I am doing:

Tuesday Aug 9, 2007. My egg crate smells like cat pound. I am
tired of stink back here. It smell better in bus station after
Urine Festival. My bladder is size of infected pumpkin. It is
now outside my stomach and i put washcloth over it.

Yaggi's cousin bought some medicated socks in Razastan and showed
them to us on his cell phone. His foot looks like infected
pumpkin yellow, brown, squishy.

I WOULD THROW RAVIOLI POOP AGAIN IF I HAD THE CHANCE!!!

With respect for Detrol and ravioli (but not poop),

Bahir Kabobby

- 211 -

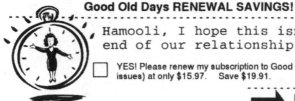

HAMOOLI KABOBBY
1413 1/2 Kenneth Rd.
#193
Glendale, CA 91201

Subscriptions
GOOD OLD DAYS MAGAZINE
House Of White Briches
PO Box 9001
Big Sandy, TX 75755-9001

Dear Good Ol' Days Magazine in Big Sandy Texas:

I once knew man named Big Sandy from Texas. 475 pounds 6 foot 11.
He painted religious scenes on white rice. It was funny to see
tiny little rice and big guy showing them to you with his fat
hands. His friend, Little Andy from Big Sandy (Texas), was 2
foot 1. he threw him against the wall and he bounced. but he was
OK. I guess he thought he was piece of rice. (Little Andy)

You say to me, "Hamooli, I hope this isn't the end of our
relationship." Of course it isn't. I am waiting for magazine
now. When will it arrive? Yes, i feel like part of your family
too (like you say) and I too enjoy reading warm nostalgic story.
That remind me of warm nostalgic story regarding infected fish I
once had as boy. I grew up in Big Sandy, Texas and my fish had an
infected gill. That fish ate nothing but Cheetos and always had
orange around its mouth. That is warm fuzzy story i wanted to
share with you, Good Ol' Days magazine. You are favorite magazine
of mine next to Turkish Mountain Biking.

Bahir did something very wrong throwing that ravioli poop inside
Dennys. Witnesses say they heard employee in Spanish accent yell
"incoming" and then they saw the poop hit wall. There was much
confusion as many ran out. Bahir had grin on his face. He yelled
"Goolab" when he threw poop . What does that mean, Big Sandy
peoples? he was Mad that he was blamed for grill he did not
steal. But that is no reason to throw ravioli poop inside Dennys.
I am waiting for September issue of Good Old Days magazine. when
will it be in my mailbox? I have another fuzzy warm story for you
about infected rodent i once knew that was on Dextrol.

Thank you,

Hamooli Kabooby

View this e-mail as Web page.

GOOD ⬧ OLD ⬧ DAYS

Dear Friends of the Good Old Days,

A Great Christmas Cookie Contest!

Remember when your grandma showed up at your house every Christmas with fresh-baked cookies?

Well, we're sure you've got a traditional holiday goody that echoes your particular family heritage -- things like fruit-filled Slovakian kolaches, spicy German pfeffernusse or crunchy Dutch speculaas.

So, here's a challenge from my friend, Pam Marra, the editor of *Town Square* magazine:

Send Pam your recipes, along with some information about where they originated and what makes them so special, and you could come up a sweet winner!

Better yet, if you've put your own, modern spin on a passed-down-to-you family favorite, that just might take you straight to the top!

There are three things we'll be looking for:

- Taste
- Appearance
- Ease of preparation

Prizes will include $150 for first place; $100 for second, and $50 for third. The winning recipes will be featured in the December issue of *Town Square*.

Be sure to follow these guidelines:

1. Provide accurate measurements of all ingredients and clear instructions for preparation.
2. We'll accept only five entries per contributor, neatly typed or printed, each on its own 8 1/2 x 11-inch piece of paper.
3. Contributor's full name, address and phone number must appear with each recipe submitted.
4. Deadline for entry is Aug. 15, 2007.

Submit recipes online at:
www.TownSquaremagazine.com/contests.html
Or mail to:
Town Square Cookie Contest
306 East Parr Road
Berne, IN 46711

*Recipes become the property of Dynamic Resource Group and may be published in a future publication.

Back to top.

Til next time,

Ken Tate
Editor,
Good Old Days®
Good Old Days® Specials
Good Old Days® Books

GEELA KABOBBY
1413 1/2 Kenneth Rd.
#193
Glendale, CA 91201

Subscriptions
GOOD OLD DAYS MAGAZINE
House Of White Briches
PO Box 9001
Big Sandy, TX 75755-9001

Dear Good Ol' Days Magazine in Big Sandy Texas:

I want to set record straight. Hamooli did not grow up in Big
Sandy, Texas and he did not have fish as boy. He has goat now
with infected teats. Not 1 teat but many teats. They are red and
blotchy and goat cries out at night for ointment. I hear goat
moans from my plastic wrap home. I cannot read my Danielle Steel
romance novels when all i vision are infected goat teats. It is
up to ME to put goo on goat. On all 8 teats. No one else will
do. I put on in counter clockwise squeeze. My life is bad.

There is no Big Sandy man or Little Andy small man. Hamooli is
sick liar! my marriage is strained. There is no rodent on
Detrol.

When will magazine come? I particularly enjoy warm nostalgic
stories. I may tell you one later about my childhood and
infected skunk i had as pet. My credit stinks. I can pay for
your magazine with other magazines.

Regards from sandy Glendale,

Geela Kabobby
Wife of liar Hamooli Kabobby

Respond by: **08/14/06**

Hamooli Kabobby   T1013 P1
1413 1/2 W Kenneth Rd # 193
Glendale CA 91201-1478

Affordable health insurance is something that can't wait.

Dear Hamooli Kabobby,

Let me pose a question to you:

If someday, you or someone you love needs medical attention, will you have the coverage you need?

It's easy to drift along, thinking everything will always be all right. And then, Hamooli Kabobby, if health problems strike—will you be taken care of?

At MEGA, we understand. That's why we've made available an affordable health insurance* plan for people who are responsible for obtaining their own health insurance.

If that includes you, here are the basics:

   • Flexible plan options to fit your budget.
   • Your choice on doctors, hospitals or other service providers.
   • No pre-certification required.

Hamooli Kabobby, I'd like to provide you with more information so that you can evaluate this program and decide for yourself if it provides the health care answers you've been looking for.

Respond to this offer today:

   • Visit our website at www.MyHealth.CompareMega.com for Rush Processing!
   • Call our Toll-Free number at 1-800-827-9990.
   • Mail the Confidential Information Request form below in the enclosed postage paid envelope.

Can you afford to wait any longer for affordable health insurance? Please complete and mail the enclosed information data card today.

Sincerely,
The MEGA Life and Health Insurance Company

P.S. Hamooli Kabobby, if you're responsible for obtaining your own health insurance, this may be the plan you're looking for. **Please respond by 08/14/06.**

Insurance plans are underwritten by The MEGA Life and Health Insurance Company. Home Office: Oklahoma City, OK. Benefits may vary by state. A licensed insurance agent will contact you regarding the details, including the exclusions and limitations. Association membership may be required. Not for sale in the state of Vermont. M-NATL0798

HAMOOLI KABOBBY
1413 1/2 Kenneth Rd.
#193
Glendale, CA 91201

MEGA LIFE & HEALTH INSURANCE CO.
9151 Grapevine HiWay
North Richland Hills, TX 76180

Dear Mega Life & Health Insurance Co.

Let me pose question to you: Do you also have car insurance?
Recently, as one who has no health insurance, I became sick. I
inhaled toxic fumes coming from fermentation of dates, figs,
hummus, chick peas, damp underwear, and cheap male perfume.

I DO have car insurance. So i went to my car and got sick in
there. I passed out in car after yelling out the name BIG SANDY.
I was treated in car by medic named Larry who leaned against me
with some hair on his arm. I filed claim with car insurance co.
they said this was not car insurance problem . They said had I
been in accident while driving I would have been covered. So I
got back into car, revved engine, and crashed car into tree. Then
i became disoriented. I stood up and yelled out; MY GRAPEFRUIT
HAS NO SQUIRT! (then i collapsed. went down like skin tag in
doctor's office.) ROY!!!

They covered my car AND my hospital stay, Mega peoples. Except, I
now do not have car insurance. Once again i ask you: Do you sell
car insurance???   They curse me in Feezi and remove me from
policy. what can we do??? I have 13 sick peoples on my hands.
some with boils and welts. One has yellow eyes and veins that
resemble mapquest direction. Can you cover me? I am ready. I
have heard good things about Mega. Hopefully its you and not the
vitamins. I once got crayon stuck in my tush.

With respect for insurance process,

Hamooli Kabobby

Because you were referred to me, I wanted to personally invite you as my VIP guest to hear my story and be trained by "5" of my personal mentors, who are some of the wealthiest self-made multi-millionaire experts in America. We will share with you our unique wealth creating secrets and strategies. As my special VIP guest, I have enclosed **two (2) complimentary tickets** and you will receive a free special edition of *"TRUMP Style Negotiation"* at the conference. The suggested tuition fee of $149 is waived for you.

yes!!!

Appearing Live: Richard Dreyfuss, Actor, Producer & Writer

At this once in a lifetime financial conference you will learn how to:
1. Regularly buy real estate for 31%-57% below value. 2. Use the 21 money-making secrets millionaires are using. 3. Slash capital gains tax to "0" when you sell real estate, stocks, or your business. 4. Lower your 2007 tax bill up to 31%. 5. Retire in 2 to 5 years with an additional cash flow of $9,100 per month. 6. Protect 100% of your personal assets from all lawsuits, liens, levies, bankruptcy, or even a divorce.

7. Get govern

8. Learn how

Turn this speci

Please give m

Looking forwa

Reed West

Reed West
President - Celebrity Conference™

See Back for Location and Date

**P.S. At The Celebrity Conference you will learn what others have paid over
$20,000 to learn. Please RSVP soon as this event will be sold out.**

P.P.S. Special Notice - free lunch provided. *Yes Again!!!*

Make January 10th the day you put your financial house in order.

HAMOOLI KABOBBY
1413 1/2 Kenneth Rd.
#193
Glendale, CA 91201

Tickets
CELEBRITY CONFERENCE
808 E.U. Valley Dr.
American Fork, UT 84003

Dear Tickets at Celebrity Conference:

Thank you for your kind invitation for you to tell me how to
become millionaire. And complimentary VIP Ticket to Celebrity
Conference. The last time i went to one of these things i fell
asleep and was not wakened till next morning by man vacuuming.

So, maybe i will attend and give another try. And Yes, I want to
meet Richard Dreyfuss!! He is my favorite actor. I saw him as
child growing up in New Tozzi in movie about people with beards
and sandals. He was covered with baking powder & had goat
ointment that he was squishing furiously. (i think it was him).

Now down to your conference. Re: Free lunch provided. Will, you
serve macaroni? When will you make the Richard Dreyfuss
introduction to me? Should i wear long pants? I have been
de-flead. Any credit for that?

Looking forward to seminar & lunch,

Hamooli Kabobby

T. ROWE PRICE INVESTMENT SERVICES, INC.

P.O. Box 17630 / Baltimore, MD / 21297–1630

May 19, 2006

Dear Hamooli Kabobby:

Whether you're saving for retirement or trying to build overall financial security, the **T. Rowe Price Equity Income Fund** (PRFDX) can help anchor your portfolio. In fact, Morningstar recently noted that it is "one of the large-value category's best options."-Morningstar, Inc. (4/10/06)*

Invest in a fund with a strong sense of value.

The Equity Income Fund uses a value-oriented strategy to invest in established companies with strong records of paying dividends. Since dividends are always a positive component of total return, they can help provide some downside protection during market declines. The fund provides a relatively conservative way to access the substantial growth potential of stocks without incurring all the risks of more aggressive stock funds. At the same time, the fund's undervalued holdings could offer attractive capital appreciation potential if they regain favor in the marketplace.

The value approach carries the risk that the market will not recognize a security's true worth for an unexpectedly long time, or that a stock judged to be undervalued may actually be appropriately priced.

Invest for long-term performance.

Investing in the fund is easy—*simply complete the Open an Account Form and return it with your check.If you want to transfer assets currently invested at another firm, also fill out the enclosed Transfer of Non-retirement Assets Form and return it.Enclosed is a profile; if you would like to receive a prospectus, please call 1-866-691-2242. The profile and prospectus include investment objectives, risks, fees, expenses, and other information that you should read and consider carefully before investing.*

If you have questions about the Equity Income Fund or any of our other 90 no-load mutual funds, call **1-866-691-2242** or visit our Web site at **troweprice.com/start**.

Sincerely,

Edward C. Bernard

Edward C. Bernard
President
T. Rowe Price Investment Services, Inc.

HAMOOLI KABOBBY
1413 1/2 Kenneth Rd.
#193
Glendale, CA 91201

EDWARD C. BERNARD
T ROWE PRICE PEOPLES
PO Box 17630
Baltimore, MD 21297-1630

Hello Edward Bernards.

Nice to hear from you again. When we last corresponded
Generalissimo Tazmak had stolen my grill and I wanted T Rowe Price
to get him involved in lot of paperwork and demote him a rank.

So when i got your most recent junk mail i was quite happy to hear
from you. When can we start addressing him as Colonelissimo
Tazmak? He should not be General in my eye but until you at T
Bone Price demote him in sea of paperwork and junk mail - i can
not do it. I must still address him as Generalissimo and that is
sad knowing that he stole grill and stole Coco from Shwarmi, MY
OWN COUSIN!!!

You know, Bernards, an old Feezian proverb states: a camel's hump
may be filled with water but is it bottled water and can it be
given out at a meeting? If you catch my drift. I know you know
what i mean. This applies to Generalissimo Tazmak 100 percent!!!
LARRY!!!

Yes, Grandfather tossed a ravioli poop inside a Dennys. But if
you look at that proverb you will see why. Grandfather Bahir has
entered dating world and I hope that works out for him. He has
picked out a dating name handle & is just waiting for approval
from dating site to meets peoples. It may be last hope for him,
this dating thing. Lets root for Bahir.

I look forward to more paperwork from you. Keep it coming!

Respectfully,

Hamooli Kabobby

T. Rowe Price
INVEST WITH CONFIDENCE

February 8, 2007

```
***********************AUTO**3-DIGIT 912
Hamooli Kabobby
1413 1/2 Kenneth Rd. 193
Glendale, CA  91201-1478
```

Dear Hamooli Kabobby:

When choosing where to invest your IRA this year, we encourage you to take a closer look at T. Rowe Price. A T. Rowe Price SmartChoice IRA is an easy yet smart solution for your retirement savings.

With a T. Rowe Price SmartChoice IRA, your savings are invested in one of our Retirement Funds, which is made up of a diversified mix of up to 14 different T. Rowe Price funds. Selecting a Retirement Fund is simple—all you do is choose the date closest to your expected year of retirement, and we do the rest.

The enclosed booklet contains everything you need to open a new account or transfer your existing IRA to T. Rowe Price. Our EasyTransfer IRA Service makes it simple to move an existing IRA to T. Rowe Price. You can also open an account online at **ira.troweprice.com**, or call our Investment Guidance Specialists at **1-866-274-9085**. They can even open your account right over the phone. *To request a prospectus, please call 1-866-274-9085 or visit ira.troweprice.com. The profile and prospectus include investment objectives, risks, fees, expenses and other information that you should read and consider carefully before investing. To invest in the funds, complete the enclosed new account form.*

Act by April 16 for 2006 tax advantages. The maximum contribution for 2006 is $4,000; $5,000 for investors who were 50 or older in 2006.

Sincerely,

Edward C. Bernard

Edward C. Bernard
President
T. Rowe Price Investment Services, Inc.

There are many considerations when planning for retirement. Your retirement needs, expenses, sources of income and available assets are some important factors for you to consider in addition to the Retirement Funds. Before investing in one of these funds, also be sure to weigh your objectives, time horizon and risk tolerance. The funds' investment in many underlying funds means that they will be exposed to the risks of different areas of the market.

HAMOOLI KABOBBY
1413 1/2 Kenneth Rd.
#193
Glendale, CA 91201

EDWARD C. BERNARD
T ROWE PRICE PEOPLES
PO Box 17630
Baltimore, MD 21297-1630

Hello Mr. Bernard, Edward C.!

I see you are still bombarding me with paperwork from T Shirt
Price. Sweet! This will surely help in demoting that miserable
Generalissimo down in rank. Keep it coming! I will show it to
him. ANDY! I have left a lot of it in his carton in backyard
(which is stinky) I can take as much mail as you can send. We
work together in this regard with Corn Rowe Price junk mail The
finest junk mail out there! OH YEAH!

Hey, what time is it there in Baltimore? it's now 2 o'clock here.

You mention Ira in your last mailing, who is that? Is he
Feezian? Ira's are usually good with money.

Bahir thinks he will meet the next Mrs. from his dating ad. Ha!
I curse my situation. He is sure he will attract lady with his
"dating handle". It smells in back of house. Real bad.

Sincerely,

Hamooli Kabobby

T. Rowe Price
INVEST WITH CONFIDENCE

March 13, 2007

Dear Hamooli Kabobby:

Having a solid cornerstone for the equity portion of your portfolio is essential, so it's important to choose a fund that offers long-term growth potential without assuming a high level of risk. For more than 55 years, the T. Rowe Price Growth Stock Fund (PRGFX) has helped thousands of investors reach their long-term goals, and it was recently included on *SmartMoney* magazine's list of "The 35 Best Mutual Funds."* In fact, it was selected as the "Top Pick" in the large-cap growth category.

Attractive long-term growth potential.

Since 1950, we've managed the Growth Stock Fund by carefully researching and choosing well-managed, established companies— both at home and, to a lesser extent, abroad— whose earnings are growing faster than inflation and the economy in general. This investment style provides long-term capital appreciation potential. And because the Growth Stock Fund invests in well-established companies, it may be a good choice for investors looking for growth potential in their portfolio without taking on more risk than necessary. Of course, all funds are subject to risk, including loss of principal.

It's easy to get started.

Investing in the fund is easy—just complete the Open an Account Form and return it with your check. If you want to transfer assets currently invested at another firm, also fill out the enclosed Transfer of Nonretirement Assets Form and return it. *Enclosed is a profile. If you would like to receive a prospectus, please call 1-866-691-2240. Each includes investment objectives, risks, fees, expenses, and other information that you should read and consider carefully before investing.*

If you have questions about the Growth Stock Fund or any of our over 90 no-load mutual funds, visit our Web site at **troweprice.com/start**, or call **1-866-691-2240**. For more in-depth assistance in choosing a fund, ask our Investment Guidance Specialists. They can help you decide if a particular fund is right for you, and can even offer guidance on your entire portfolio.

Sincerely,

Edward C. Bernard

Edward C. Bernard
President
T. Rowe Price Investment Services, Inc.

---

* *SmartMoney* selected funds from seven investment categories based on performance (before and after taxes), low turnover, and expenses as of 11/30/06. The Growth Stock Fund was selected as one of five funds in the large-cap growth category.
Source: *SmartMoney* 2007 "35 Best Mutual Funds." *SmartMoney* is a registered trademark of SmartMoney, a joint venture of Dow Jones & Company, Inc and Hearst[SM] Partnership.

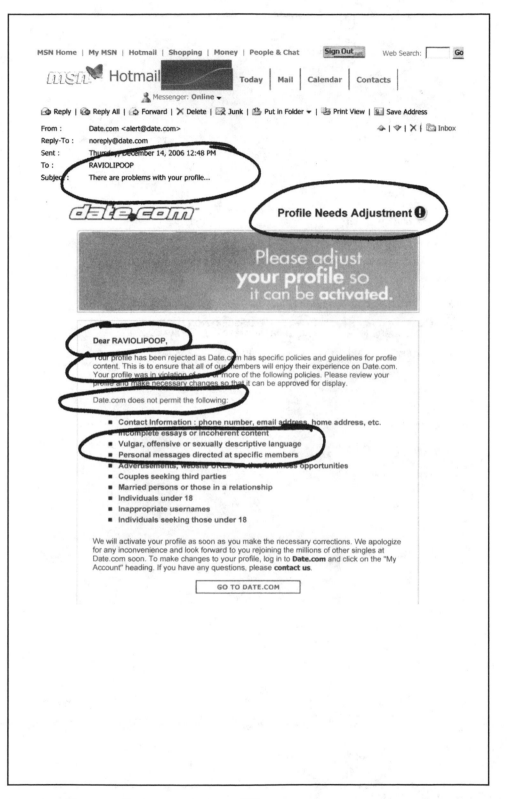

msn. Hotmail   Today | Mail | Calendar | Contacts

Messenger: Online ▾

Reply | Reply All | Forward | ✕ Delete | Junk | Put in Folder ▾ | Print View | Save Address

From :   Date.com <alert@date.com>
Reply-To :   noreply@date.com
Sent :   Thursday, December 14, 2006 12:48 PM
To :   RAVIOLIPOOP
Subject :   There are problems with your profile...

date.com   **Profile Needs Adjustment** ❗

Please adjust your profile so it can be activated.

Dear RAVIOLIPOOP,

Your profile has been rejected as Date.com has specific policies and guidelines for profile content. This is to ensure that all of our members will enjoy their experience on Date.com. Your profile was in violation of one or more of the following policies. Please review your profile and make necessary changes so that it can be approved for display.

Date.com does not permit the following:

- Contact Information : phone number, email address, home address, etc.
- Incomplete essays or incoherent content
- Vulgar, offensive or sexually descriptive language
- Personal messages directed at specific members
- Advertisements, website URLs or other business opportunities
- Couples seeking third parties
- Married persons or those in a relationship
- Individuals under 18
- Inappropriate usernames
- Individuals seeking those under 18

We will activate your profile as soon as you make the necessary corrections. We apologize for any inconvenience and look forward to you rejoining the millions of other singles at **Date.com** soon. To make changes to your profile, log in to **Date.com** and click on the "My Account" heading. If you have any questions, please **contact us**.

GO TO DATE.COM

BAHIR KABOBBY
1413 1/2 Kenneth Rd.
#193
Glendale, CA 91201

DATE.COM PEOPLES
1521 Alton Rd #626
Miami Beach, FL 33139

Dear Date.Dot Com Peoples:

HASSELAMMM!!!   ZALLEUMMM!!!   SAHSHEEYAMM!!   (!!!!)
MASHESHAAM!!! KALLEUMMM!! HASSEMEEE!!!   KABABALLAHH!!!

AHSHEEYAMM!!   (!!!!)   KABULADAH!!! SHALEAAAMMM!!   (???)
KABIBIBAMAA!! VULGAR!   INAPPROPRIATE USERNAMES!!   HALLIUUMMA!!
SALEEM!!

Sincerely,

Bahir Kabobby
Raviolipoop

KABOOM!

GEELA & HAMOOLI KABOBBY
REQUEST YOUR PRESENCE
AT WEDDING OF

COCO LaBOY

TO

GENERALISSIMO TAZMAK

IN OUR BACKYARD
1413 1/2 KENNETH RD #193
GLENDALE, CALIFORNIA 91201

SATURDAY
JANUARY 5TH, 2007
5:P:M

Join us afterwards for a Ravioli Dinner
Prepared by Grandfather Bahir

Dear Coco,

Eeeeeeeeeeeeeeeeeeeee!

Is there anything more EXHILARATING than
being engaged?

You've learned to use your left hand to perform
even mundane daily tasks (like brushing your
teeth), just so you can watch that ring sparkle...

You unabashedly daydream during work meetings,
doodling "Mrs. So-and-So" in your note pad or
sketching out elaborate renderings of your
"dream dress"...

And wherever you go, you want to shout from the
rooftops: "I'M GETTING MARRIED!!!"

As if being engaged wasn't fun enough on its
own...

You also have access to my FABULOUS online
marketplace for "brides on a budget" -
Free Wedding Classifieds!

Have you checked it out yet?

It's chock-full of amazing deals on everything
from dresses and accessories to gifts, caterers
and honeymoon packages.

And on it, I've found some FANTASTIC ways for
you to let EVERYONE know that you're the bride!

Now remember, these deals are just the
ICING ON THE CAKE!

There are BARGAINS GALORE to be found on
Free Wedding Classifieds!

So grab that mouse and click on:

http://www.FreeWeddingClassifieds.com

(Yes, you can use your LEFT HAND.)

I'll write you again soon.

Your Friend,

- S
Beverly Hills, CA

P.S. Don't forget, Free Wedding Classifieds is a
great place to sell your stuff (and make back some
cash) after your wedding is over, too!

COCO LABOY-TAZMAK
1413 1/2 Kenneth Rd.
#193
Glendale, CA 91201

S WEDDINGS
Beverly Hills, CA 90211

Dear S

Hiiiiiiiiiiiiiiii! I am engaged to a wonderful military man. He
is a General although I suspect soon he will be demoted to a
Colonel if T Rowe Price has their way. They are involving him in
ALOT of paperwork as I speak.

I am now calling myself Coco LaBoy-Tazmak in honor of the
Generalissimo Tazmak. I will proudly take his name and live in
bliss as others can only look in. **(3 more days until our
wedding!!!)**

Yes I need a wedding dress. Has anyone ever been married in
pistachio? (white is so 2007) I will wear it with my red Wizard
Of Oz shoes & stretched bicycle shorts underneath. The General
has big hands and I want Yaggi & Shwarmi to be jealous. They eye
me from their fig carton where they have started living together.
(Disgustiiiing!)

Yaggi said he went to a conference and he spoke to Richard
Dreyfuss and they ate macaroni together. He told Yaggi he was
coming to my wedding. I don't even believe it was Richard
Dryfuss. He said it was some Brazilian man he ate macaroni with.
Is that Richard Dryness to you?

One of my all time favorite Richard Dryness movies was BATMAN 12.
Where he played The Nibbler. The Nibbler terrorized Batman by
nibbling on carrot sticks and celery stalks. I guess that could
drive anyone crazy, S. Even Batman. I also liked him in "The
Goodbye Gator" where he played Rudy the man with an appendage
growing out of his thigh and covered in baking powder.

Bahir is making some food for our wedding. He cooks with ravioli
ALOT.

Soon to be a missus,

Coco LaBoy-Tazmak

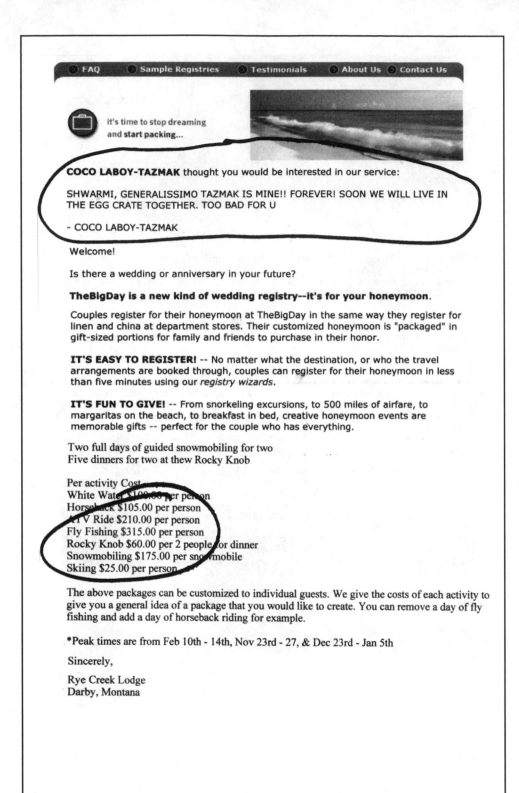

it's time to stop dreaming
and **start packing**...

COCO LABOY-TAZMAK thought you would be interested in our service:

SHWARMI, GENERALISSIMO TAZMAK IS MINE!! FOREVER! SOON WE WILL LIVE IN
THE EGG CRATE TOGETHER. TOO BAD FOR U

- COCO LABOY-TAZMAK

Welcome!

Is there a wedding or anniversary in your future?

TheBigDay is a new kind of wedding registry--it's for your honeymoon.

Couples register for their honeymoon at TheBigDay in the same way they register for
linen and china at department stores. Their customized honeymoon is "packaged" in
gift-sized portions for family and friends to purchase in their honor.

IT'S EASY TO REGISTER! -- No matter what the destination, or who the travel
arrangements are booked through, couples can register for their honeymoon in less
than five minutes using our *registry wizards*.

IT'S FUN TO GIVE! -- From snorkeling excursions, to 500 miles of airfare, to
margaritas on the beach, to breakfast in bed, creative honeymoon events are
memorable gifts -- perfect for the couple who has everything.

Two full days of guided snowmobiling for two
Five dinners for two at thew Rocky Knob

Per activity Cost
White Water $100.00 per person
Horseback $105.00 per person
ATV Ride $210.00 per person
Fly Fishing $315.00 per person
Rocky Knob $60.00 per 2 people for dinner
Snowmobiling $175.00 per snowmobile
Skiing $25.00 per person

The above packages can be customized to individual guests. We give the costs of each activity to
give you a general idea of a package that you would like to create. You can remove a day of fly
fishing and add a day of horseback riding for example.

*Peak times are from Feb 10th - 14th, Nov 23rd - 27, & Dec 23rd - Jan 5th

Sincerely,

Rye Creek Lodge
Darby, Montana

COCO LABOY-TAZMAK
1413 1/2 Kenneth Rd.
#193
Glendale, CA 91201

RESERVATIONS
RYE CREEK LODGE
Darby Montana

Dear Reservation Clerk Rye Bread Lodge:

Thank you for addressing me as Coco LaBoy-Tazmak. That is soon to
be my new name. My impending marriage is recognized in 14 states
(and one motel. in Sacramento). Montana is one of the
recognizing states and that is where we will honeymoon. All shots
are completed, except tetanus & VH1.

We want to go Snowmobiling, rocky knobing, and fly fishing like
your ad says. I understand Richard Dreyfuss will be there and eat
macaroni and marry us off. (that's what I heard. Sure.) My
fave RD movie is ""Superman 9" where he played The Snacker. He
snacked on avocados and melon cubes. How do we get to Rye Bread
Lodge? We will leave Hamooli's backyard on Kenneth Road in a hail
of rice and good wishes and head straight for Knob Creek and you,
Mr. Rye.

First we will have a fried pepper spoomengelli at the Barking Frog
Restaurant. I lost a bandaid there once. **2 more days until we
are married!!!**

Respect for the sanctimony of marriage,

Coco LaBoy-Tazmak

Muldoon's Men's Wear

My Account | Account History | Login | Logout | My Cart | My Wish List

SIGN UP!
JOIN OUR MAILING LIST

Search...

Shop by brand

Home

Shop By Category
Holiday Shopping
Newest Items
Clearance Items
Nightwear
Underwear
Accessories
Footwear
Items Under $20
Formal Wear
Custom Clothing

Shop By Size
Regular Sizes
Big & Tall Sizes
Short & Small
  • Dress Slacks
  • Casual Slacks
  • Dress Shirts
  • Suits
  • Blazers
  • Outerwear
  • Jeans
  • Hosiery/Socks

Additional Links
Souvenirs
Favorite Links
Fax Order Form
Contact Us

Thanksgiving 5-Day Sale
20% Off

Sale Va
Nov. 22 - 2
20% Off Discou
In Shopping

Clearance Items
Save Upto 87%
See Our
Clearance Items
Click Here!

Bainbridge
1/2 Off
All Remaining
Slacks
Click Here!

Perry

home > short & small > hosiery/socks

HOSIERY / SOCKS

Vannucci Diabetic Socks - Small Man
Style #SL-101
Available In Black, Navy, Brown & Charcoal
Muldoon's Price $7.50

HAMOOLI KABOBBY
1413 1/2 Kenneth Rd.
#193
Glendale, CA 91201

MULDOONS MENS WEAR
1506 S. Hastings Way
Eau Claire, WI 54701

Dear Muldoons Mens Wear Peoples:

Thank you for another newsletter and your fine products. Yes, I
want Vanucci diabetic sock. Why? I don't know. But I want it.
NOW!!

The big wedding is 2 days!!! and relatives have begun arriving.
By the way, Muldoons, my sister Feroozi has got medical clearance
to attend. Her hairy mole is under control. She sends her wishes
and wants to meet you when diabetic sock arrive. Yaggi's daughter
Asma has been here already 20 minutes. We are all catching up on
family fun. Asma told me Zakeesta has many bites on her aerolas.

Now down to your sock stretching in your last letter. I stretched
my sock out like you said. I have size 19 foot and your sock is
size 6 1/2. I finally got it onto my foot. I have no movement in
my leg now from my ankle down. Just tingling and a "dead foot"
feeling. When do i take sock off?

Backyard wedding is fast approaching and Richard Dreyfuss will be
here to officiate and screen his movie "THE NIBBLER BARFS UP
CARROT." (i think that is title)

After i marry that wretched Coco LaBoy off he will live away from
here with that thief relative of mine Tazmak. I CAN'T WAIT TO RID
MYSELF OF THESE 2 PEOPLES!!! Send me diabetic sock. In blue. My
leg has no feeling as we speak. (and is blue also)

Respect for your products,

Hamooli Kabobby

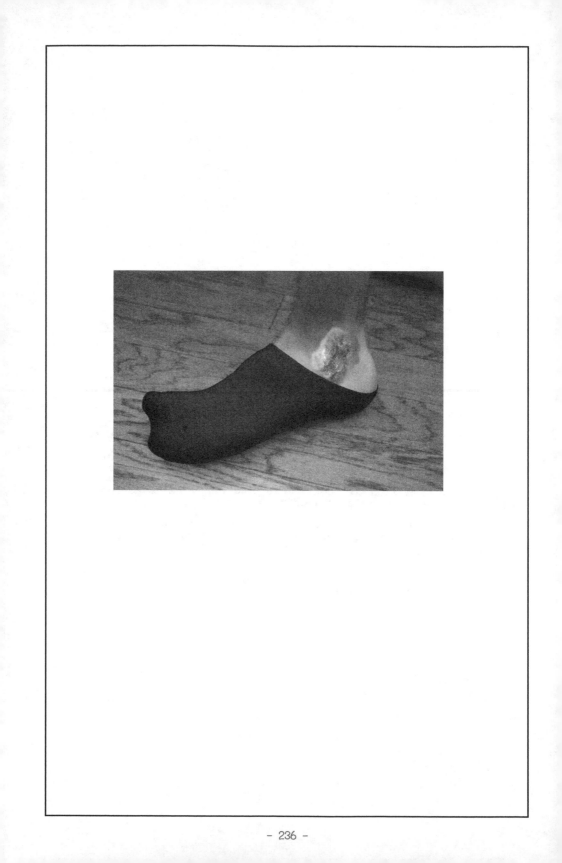

MULDOON'S MEN'S WEAR, INC.

February 13, 2007

Dear Hamooli Kabobby,

Thanks for your inquiry. All the items you mentioned can be seen on our website: http://www.muldoons.com/muldoons/

Sincerely,

Big, Tall
Short or Small
We Fit Them All

Since 1950

Muldoon's MEN'S WEAR
Where People of Good Taste Shop

1506 S. Hastings Way
Eau Claire, WI 54701-4463

(715) 832-3502 • Fax (715) 832-6798 • (800) 942-0783

muldoons.com

1506 SOUTH HASTINGS WAY • EAU CLAIRE, WI • 54701
PHONE: (715) 832-3502 • FAX: (715) 832-6798

Sent :   Saturday, December 9, 2006 6:17 PM

Subject :   Your Stop Snoring Newsletter

Hello, Scott Kabibby

Welcome to the Stop Snoring newsletter! I'm so glad you've joined us! I hope our information will be helpful to you!

My main reason for creating this newsletter was to give you all the stop snoring knowledge you require to improve your life.

You'll receive an exclusive tip or article each week like the one below, Scott Kabibby

Whenever we send out this newsleter, we will always ask you to go to a specially created website to read the information we send.

This allows us to keep the information right up to date, and helps you find the information on the internet more effectively.

To get to this exclusive website all you need to do is put the following URL into your browser.
http://www.the-news-source.com/30-1/stop-snoring/1

Try it now and you will see an example of the stop snoring news and information available.

Again, I appreciate your joining us – and we'll see you in a few days!

Well, thanks again for joining us,
Take care

16 Sandown House, 1 High Street
Esher, Surrey KT10 9SL United Kingdom

SCOTT KABOBBY
1413 1/2 Kenneth Rd.
#193
Glendale, CA 91201

SERVICE
STOP SNORING NEWSLETTER
16 Sandown House, 1 High Street
Esher, Surrey KT 10 9SL United Kingdom

Dear Stop Snoring People:

My name is Kabobby. Not KABIBBY. You wrote me as Scott Kabibby.
I am Scott Kabobby. But that is OK. I am dealing with it, what
with all on my plate right now. I hope I am thinking clearly for
the wedding which is **the day after tomorrow.**

I understand all will be there: I will shave my back and adjust
my hair strips and only smoke 2 cigarettes at once for the big
event to be held in our backyard. The hair strips on my back itch
so much i can only scream out in insane asylum yelling.

The electricity situation with Bahir is bad. I see sparks shoot
out of a plug that Bahir has been working on to plug in his TV
set. There is a problem there. I keep telling people that.
Hello!!! Is anyone listening?!!!! HIS ELECTRICAL TV PLUG SHOOTS
OUT ELECTRICITY!

With only **1 day left** I hope this big event comes off ok. I hope
my hair, snoring, bed wetting, back hairs, dementia barking, &
cursing slurs at others are kept at bay until all guests leave.

Yes i snore! But i can't get to sleep so i just stand there and
snore. is that bad, Snorer Man? You are the snoring expert. I
am fully awake, standing, and snoring. What will become of me?

Sincerely,

Scott Kabobby
(cough 10% gone)

YOUR ACCOUNT
› SIGN IN

SEARCH [ ] GO

SHOPPI
0 item
check

E-mail
Newsletter

Place a
Catalog Order

Shop Our
Virtual Catalog

FREE Delivery
Advantage Club℠

About Us   FAQ's   Fit Chart   FREE Catalog   Affiliate Program   Email-A-Friend   unde

Suits
Underwear
Woven Shirts
Knit Shirts
Sweaters
Sets
Outerwear
Leather
Jackets
Jeans
Pants
Shorts
Swimwear
Activewear
Lounge
Shoes
Accessories
Skincare
Join Our Clubs
On Sale Now!

Underwear

Palermo Mesh Bikini Brief
FEATUREDPRODUCT

Thongs
Bikinis
Briefs
Boxer Briefs
Boxers
Problem Solvers
Jocks
Undershirts
Contours

COCO LABOY-TAZMAK
1413 1/2 Kenneth Rd.
#193
Glendale, CA 91201

INTERNATIONAL MALE
C/O Hanover Direct
1500 Harbor Blvd.
Weehawken, NJ 07086

Hello International Male!

Who is in that ad??? Is his name Dejuan from Squinch??? I
believe I recognize him (Even after 4 rum and cokes). I am
allowed to contact others. My marriage is only recognized in 14
states (and 1 motel). The other 36 states this marriage not
recognized!!

Is his name Kurt? It's either Kurt or Dejuan. Tell me,
International Male. Question: If I cruise near your address on
Harbor Blvd in Weehawken at 9 p:m on Saturday, Jan 6th, will I be
harmed in any way? Ridiculed? Disrespected and verbally shouted
at? Ooooh.

I may be having buyers remorse over this marriage tomorrow. **1 day
to go!!!! Ohmygosh!!** Is there anything that can save me???
Maybe some gift from heaven to stop it. I know Richard D. is
coming and bringing a macaroni dish and all but....is
Generalissimo Tazmak the right man for me, International Male?

If I eat another Turkish Apricot I will puke. My butt looks like
car wash flaps from all that's going on. (soapy & damp & flappy)

I so want to get away from this backyard. What will happen to
me????

Thank you,

Coco LaBoy-?Tazmak

NEPTUNE SOCIETY

Area Representative
4312 Woodman Ave. 3rd Floor. Sherman Oaks, CA 91423

CALL ME

Ms. Kabobby:

I am the area representative for The Neptune Society in your community and as such am requesting to arrange a fifteen minute appointment to explain detailed and specific information on the varied aspects of our program (benefits-financial-etc.) and to answer any questions you may have. If you wish to enroll, I do the legal paperwork for you (15 Minutes). If not, I am on my way to my next appointment. No obligation – no pressure.

By mailing you this enclosed information, my ability to share with you specifics on our program is limited. This is not like comparing benefits and cost on auto insurance or buying a vacuum cleaner. Most people want all the information they can gather before making such a major decision. The information I am mailing you is just some of our basic marketing material.

If you know cremation is the path you are choosing, the three reasons for enrolling now are that the price is immediately frozen and will never go up for you, at the time of need EVERYTHING is taken care of beforehand so your loved ones are spared the pain and distress of making arrangements at such a traumatic time, and you are covered anywhere in the WORLD whether traveling or should you relocate.

If you feel you have sufficient information and wish to enroll or would like to make an appointment to discuss your options, please call me **or fill out the form.**

NEPTUNE SOCIETY®
4312 Woodman Avenue, 3rd Floor
Sherman Oaks, CA 91423

US POSTAGE
$ 00.63
FIRST CLASS
Mailed From 91423
02/18/2007
031A 0002302228

Geela Kabobby
1413 ½ Kenneth Road # 193
Glendale, CA 91201

91201+1421

GEELA KABOBBY
1413 1/2 Kenneth Rd.
#193
Glendale, CA 91201

Cremate Specialist
NEPTUNE SOCIETY
4312 Woodman Ave
Sherman Oaks, CA 91423

Dear Neptune Society mans.

Now. I want to go now. crumble me into ash. My credit is
terrible. My marriage is horrible. Hamooli smells & has boils.
My son Scott's teats are enormous, he has man whoppers. his grey
cigarette lips bad. He snores when he is awake and has level 3
dementia. My baby Maheeni is almost 500 pounds. She eats loafs
of bread all day. Readers Digest hates me.

I am ready for cremation, Neptune peoples & Mr. Cremation.
Kachunk, kakachunka, kakachunka!! Dance to the beat.

When? Who will pick me up? In my driveway. Clear away the filth
and take me away for ash ceremony. **Wedding in 1 day!!!** I puke.

With respect for the unliving,

Geela Kabobby
Geela Kabobby

NEPTUNE SOCIETY®
AMERICA'S CREMATION SPECIALISTS®
TOLL FREE: (800) NEPTUNE

Geela Kabobby
1413 1/2 W Kenneth Rd
Glendale CA 91201-1478

June 15, 2007

Dear Geela Kabobby,

We are writing you this letter as a courtesy to let you know that effective September 1, 2007 the Neptune Society prearrangement plan prices must increase. We are facing a lot of pressure to increase the price but feel an obligation to remind those that were interested at the current pricing so you can freeze today's price now!

The second issue we want to remind you of is that we now have a significant savings for all Veterans of our armed forces. This benefit may not have been available at the time you requested information.

This is a courtesy notification to give you this opportunity to take care of your family at the lowest cost. You will avoid any emotional or economic pressure being placed on your family at their time of loss.

Please take care of this issue in one of two ways

　1. Use the enclosed Payment Options form and mail it back to us. We will complete the paperwork and mail it to you.

　2. Call us toll-free at 1-800-Neptune (1-800-637-8863)

Thank you for trusting Neptune and thank you for taking the time to get this difficult issue behind you!

Yours Sincerely,

The Neptune Society

p.s. This courtesy offer is being sent to those who have had prior contact with our Society. If it has reached you at a sensitive time, we sincerely apologize. The Neptune Society is not affiliated with any traditional funeral homes or cemeteries.

GEELA KABOBBY
1413 1/2 Kenneth Rd.
#193
Glendale, CA 91201

Cremation President
NEPTUNE SOCIETY
4312 Woodman Ave
Sherman Oaks, CA 91423

Dear Cremation President, Neptunes Society.

Thank you for writing back to me with cremation price freezings.
I was worried about this. Can you just freeze price like that?

We must be discreet because this is really for Generalissimo
Tazmak. Tazmak needs to be cremated. Taxidermy not an option.
according to taxidermy board.

How much? When do we start? I would like nothing better then to
display Tazmak in urn on shelf next to knick knack from Six Flags
Over Memphis where I got diarrhea there once. (Ride jerked me up
too much)

Hamooli does not know. Busy with wedding. Can I pay in Readers
Digest Happy Money?

Respect for dead,

Geela Kabobby

Latina Order Acknowledgment

P.O. Box 37794, Boone, IA 50037-0794

DESCRIPTION 12 issues	PAY THIS AMOUNT $11.97	REPLY BY: 01/05/07

☐

☐ Payment enclosed
(payable to LATINA magazine)

☐ Visa   ☐ MasterCard   ☐ AmEx

Card # _____   Exp. Date _____

Signature _____

GENERALISSIMO TAZMAK KABOB
  193
1413 1/2 W KENNETH RD
GLENDALE   CA 91201-1478

LMV321

www.latina.com   Detach and mail top portion with your payment.

¡Gracias! Thank you for ordering *Latina!*

Dear Generalissimo Tazmak Kabob,

We have received your order for LATINA. Welcome!

LATINA is created by Latinas for Latinas like you! The pages of LATINA are a celebration of how incredible it is to be Latina today.

Please take a moment to check your name and address above, mark any necessary corrections, and mail the Acknowledgment form in the envelope provided. As soon as we receive your payment, we'll start your subscription and **rush** your FREE GIFT!

Thank you for joining us. We're delighted to welcome you as part of the fabulous LATINA familia!

¡Bienvenida!

Jennifer Schulties

Jennifer Schulties
Customer Care Director

P.S. Don't forget to take advantage of our special offer for additional issues at great savings!

P.P.S. Your **FREE GIFT** will be on its way to you as soon as we receive your payment.

GENERALISSIMO TAZMAK
1413 1/2 Kenneth Rd.
#193
Glendale, CA 91201

Subscriptions
LATINA MAGAZINE
PO Box 37794
Boone, IA 50037

Help Me Latina Magazine.

My name is not Kabob. You addressed me as Kabob. I AM
GENERALISSIMO TAZMAK! FULL MILITARY COMMANDER. G-4 FOOD
INSPECTOR PET GROOM SECTOR. In my country I was L7 Grade 19b
organizer. I did for 34 years, working in accounting position. I
have 24 years mathematics specializing in Yuro numbers in dining
specter. GYRO!! (sorry; I yell foods out) I was level 12 for 9
years and once held title of Commander Ganoush for 10 months.
SPINACH PITA!!!

I am not gay. I only marrying Coco LaBoy to gain citizenship of
U.S. But I detest it. I want Latin womens! **The marriage is
tomorrow** and I have my gift for Hamooli. But I can't go through
with this!!! When will first issue arrive? I DO not HAVE $11.97.
Where will i get it???.

Please refer to me as Colonelissimo Tazmak after 3rd issue. I
have been demoted which takes effect in 19 days. In my country I
was a military detente leader commanding over 300,000
mathematicians in food industry dealing with high government
ketchup. I was responsible for Sun Program getting a Bazzarian on
the Sun in clean socks. I once held title of Larry for 9 weeks.
Here i am now rank lower thanks to paperworks from Edwards Bernard
the T Rowe mans. Are their many fold out pages in your Latina
magazine?

I pray something will change the course and I do not have to go
through with **wedding tomorrow** to the sickening small man - Coco
Laboy-Tazmak Kabob who has taken my proud Terzazzian name and
placed it on his Wisconsin street trash buttocks. **Tomorrow is
wedding day. 19 hours to go as i write this**, Latina magazine.
What is my free gift? Will it smell?

Hurt,

Generalissimo Tazmak

LMV 00 1738 0072 B0649IQ04 06 02/08/07 12   XLM3   1,247

▪Latina. | SUBSCRIPTION INVOICE

P.O. Box 37794, Boone, IA 50037-0794

DESCRIPTION	PAY THIS AMOUNT	REPLY BY:
12 ISSUES	$11.97	03/09/07

LMV32245

☐

PAYMENT OVERDUE

☐ Payment enclosed
(payable to LATINA magazine)

☐ Visa ☐ MasterCard ☐ AmEx

Card #_____ Exp. Date_____

Signature_____

Generalissimo Tazmak Kabob
   193
1413 1/2 W Kenneth Rd
GLENDALE   CA 91201-1478
IIdmmIIuIdIIImmIIuIIdIdIIuIIddIdIdIdIdI

----

www.latina.com   Detach and mail top portion with your payment.

FOURTH NOTICE

MEMO TO: GENERALISSIMO TAZMAK KABOB
FROM: CREDIT DEPT.

YOUR ACCOUNT IS OVERDUE. YOUR LATINA SUBSCRIPTION
HAS BEEN SUSPENDED DUE TO NONPAYMENT.

ACT NOW TO RESUME SERVICE AND ASSURE YOUR GOOD
CREDIT STANDING. PLEASE SEND PAYMENT WITH THE
ATTACHED INVOICE IN THE ENVELOPE PROVIDED.

YOUR SUBSCRIPTION WILL BE REINSTATED IF YOUR PAYMENT
ARRIVES BY 03/09/07 - AND YOU WILL RECEIVE THE BALANCE
OF THE ISSUES YOU ORDERED.

> THANK YOU
> KAREN MAYAL
> COLLECTION MANAGER

P.S. IF YOU'VE ALREADY MAILED YOUR PAYMENT, THANK YOU,
AND PLEASE DISREGARD THIS NOTICE.

$11.97
WILL Mail
to Latina Magazine

Radio Free Asia

Cantonese

2006.11.27

与您共享新闻自由

安徽十名检察部门官员持伪造证件前往芬兰被遣返

2006.11.24

安徽省十名反贪污官员，本周初声称因公务前往芬兰，但入境时遭芬兰边防人员发现持伪造邀请信，把他们遣返中国。中国大使馆承认伪造邀请信事件，对此表示遗憾。芬兰边防人员则说，中国官员利用公费旅游已很平常。

北京高法周五驳回程翔上诉

2006.11.24

北京市高级人民法院周五驳回新加坡《海峡时报》东亚首席特派员程翔的上诉，维持原审法院的裁决。程翔家属对判决感到愤怒。中国法律学者指判决令人心寒。

高智晟的妻子耿和被警察殴打

2006.11.24

中国艾滋病维权人士，高智晟夫妇的朋友胡佳对本台粤语组表示，周五中午接到耿和给他的电话，指她外出时被两个跟踪的国保警察殴打。耿和被打得牙齿松动，满口是血，手指甲被打翻，衣服也被撕破了。

陈光诚的律师李方平再次与陈光诚见面

2006.11.24

山东失明维权人士陈光诚的律师李方平已抵达沂南,为下周一案件重审作好准备。他分别与陈光诚及三名主要证人会面，但对于证人届时能否顺利出庭作证仍有忧虑。而陈光诚就对重审结果持乐观的态度。

山东济南维权村民代表被判刑引发警民冲突

2006.11.24

山东省济南市槐荫区一名村民代表，因率领村民维权而被控"妨碍公务"罪，被法庭判入狱一年零九个月。六百多名村民包围村委办事处要求放人，受到近千名防暴警察武力镇压，冲突中多名村民被打伤。

HAMOOLI KABOBBY
1413 1/2 Kenneth Rd.
#193
Glendale, CA 91201

RADIO FREE ASIA CANTONESE
2025 M St NW #300
Washington DC 20036

Dear Radio Free Asia Cantonese,

I believe you misspelled a character. 警察殴打   **Today is the
day!!! The Generalissimo Tazmak-Coco LaBoy Wedding in my
backyard. What wedding? It never came off. THE EVENT:**
COLONELissimo Tazmak presented me with a wedding gift as the
"father" of the bride. (I was to give away Coco) The gift was:
MY GRILL! The thief stole it, hid it, cast aspersions on my own
grandfather Bahir who went berserk TWICE, then gave back to me as
wedding present. The nerve!. At the moment that Tazmak and Coco
were to become man and man....Bahir plugged the grill into A:
faulty wet socket with B: frayed electrical cord.

KABOOB! KABOBBY KABLOOEY! Explosion! Every piece of junk mail
ever sent to 1413 1/2 Kenneth Rd. Glendale, Ca 91201 went up in
the sky. All the credit card applications, mortgage requests,
unpaid magazines, investment crap mail, stupid junk email for
dryer products & teeth whitening, Penn Foster school garbage,
Bostisol mailings, all came down. On everyone. Every guest
there, Me, Geela, Tahini, Baby Maheeni, Scott, Grandfather Bahir,
Cousin Shwarmi, Sister Feroozi, Yaggi, Asma, Zakeesta, Fasheema,
Yimmee, Kajian Petgroomer, Bernard Edwards all ran for their lives
as my entire backyard went up in junk mail hell. I thought i
heard Richard Dreyfuss moaning in pile of wood that was once my
house. I heard tiny gnawing and saw Richard Dreyfuss twisted in
there with macaroni smeared on his face. (It may have been The
Nibbler instead of him)

THE END: Luckily the hated Coco LaBoy saved us. He carried
everyone to safety away from junk mail rubbish on top of us all.
And had the marriage gone off i would welcome him to Kabobby
family as my son-n-law. (But it did not) so now he is to be gone.
Forever! Oh. And Colonelissimo Tazmak ended up in his own jail
cell, my grill's iron bars clamping him shut in. He ended up in
his own prison. Ha Ha Ha Ha Ha!!! So this junk mail means what?
Nothing. Just a pile of trash on my family.

Respectfully,

Hamooli Kabobby

EPILOGUES *

* BECAUSE JUNK MAIL NEVER ENDS

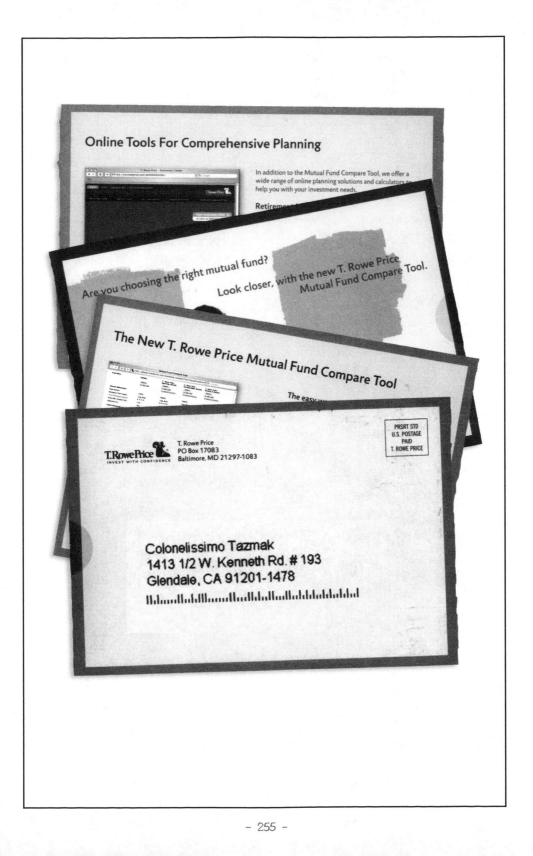

Online Tools For Comprehensive Planning

In addition to the Mutual Fund Compare Tool, we offer a wide range of online planning solutions and calculators to help you with your investment needs.

Retiremen

Are you choosing the right mutual fund?

Look closer, with the new T. Rowe Price Mutual Fund Compare Tool.

The New T. Rowe Price Mutual Fund Compare Tool

The easy

T. Rowe Price
PO Box 17083
Baltimore, MD 21297-1083

T. Rowe Price
INVEST WITH CONFIDENCE

PRSRT STD
U.S. POSTAGE
PAID
T. ROWE PRICE

Colonelissimo Tazmak
1413 1/2 W. Kenneth Rd. # 193
Glendale, CA 91201-1478

DEDICATION

To Justin Siegel

Just a solid guy. You are missed. I so enjoyed being around you.
I think of you. So you are still here in that regard. Your parents are
beautiful. Sharon & Lou. Lou, I always miss you. Still. Justin, you were
wonderful for so many lives.

ACKNOWLEDGEMENTS

I wish to give a thank you, shout out, hoo-ha, to the following:

Rita Marder (Every day you are still here), Morris Marder (a joy to have here), Alan Marder, Barry Marder, Dr. Melvin Weisberg, Jeanne Schwartz, Marilyn, Sloppy, John, Justin Deutsch, Cookie, Lou, Bert & Donald Saltzburg, Hy & Annette Marder, Nancy Abrams, Michael Marder, Peanut, Sun Ray, Johnny Dark (fabulous talent & friend) Dr. Marty Weisberg, Cele, George, Dee, Hershel Pearl, Marty Rosenthal, Sam Dansky, Karen.

Phyllis Murphy needs to be singled out. That is why she has her own line. I AM SINGLING YOU OUT!!! THANK YOU!!!!

Dan Strone is a fabulous agent. None finer. (That includes Ceylon and the Province of Puerto Rico) Stephanie in Dan's Office, thanx for all the paperwork help.

Scott Rubin, Marcy Goot at the National Lampoon - Masters at what they do. Scott - I will always love the Ernie Ladd line. Always.

Dr. Mark Gerard, Dr. Douglas Schreck, Dr. Michael Robbins, Mimi, Vicki the Dental Hygienist, Dr. Jeana Libed (my toe), Dr. Jon Vogel, Neil Meyer, Mike Shutello, Lindora Weight Clinics - Bea and the rest, Eric Bjorgum (The Norweigian Noodge), Staff at Evergreen Retirement Home.

Linda Shaw, Ann Economus-Hunt, Rikki Brothers, Fred & Lori Snyder, Carol Lynn Tabas, Renee Carter.

Allison Acken, Bonni Banyard, Aleshia Brevard, Windy Buhler, Candace Dickerson, Joyce Eyler, Jean Gennis, Susan Kamei, Susan Katz, Kristen Kirkham, Jeff Klayman, Andrea Lindsey, Jeanne Michels, Heidi Rufli, Paul Sand, Mo Stewart, Susan Trabosh and Stephan Yarian.

And of course...Jerry Seinfeld, a giant of a human being. Maybe even bigger then that. An angel with wings. (A Platinum Club, Diamond 4 Star, Gold Circle Cul De Sac Award to you. There is no higher award in the Real Estate world.)